The History, Theory and Criticism of Architecture

THE HISTORY, THEORY AND CRITICISM OF ARCHITECTURE

Papers from the

1964 AIA-ACSA TEACHER SEMINAR

edited by

MARCUS WHIFFEN

with a foreword by

BUFORD L. PICKENS

THE M.I.T. PRESS
THE MASSACHUSETTS INSTITUTE OF TECHNOLOGY
Cambridge, Massachusetts

PRINTED BY THE CRANBROOK PRESS, BLOOMFIELD HILLS, MICHIGAN

FOREWORD

by BUFORD L. PICKENS

Since the first AIA-ACSA Teacher Seminar, held in Cambridge, Massachusetts in the summer of 1956, successive program committees have attempted annually to confront the
participants with an urgent theme related intimately to the
teaching and directly to the practice of architecture. In an
effort to keep abreast of the times, they have sometimes selected
areas so comprehensive that the subjects were difficult to define
and discuss in meaningful relation to either the profession or
the schools. With increasing courage, fortified by the successes
as well as the mistakes of the past, the committees have gradually sharpened the focus of seminar assignments, narrowing
from the broad range of the entire curriculum, or man's total
environment, down to specific problems in depth, chosen from
one subject area. What began as a general professional *institute*
has evolved in theme and format to something that can be more
accurately described as a *seminar*.

Although the objective may never be fully reached, the programming has been directed less and less toward presenting a
constellation of "stars", lecturing to a passive audience—assumed to be neophytes. Instead, and because of the rising interest, the programs have increasingly been designed to encourage the assembled teachers and teacher-architects to play an
active role in the proceedings. Thus, problems arising from
teaching suggest themes which have potentials for the improvement of architecture through education. The ideal seminar
might very well have no "stars", and depend upon prepared
and articulate participants who have varied experience and
positive views.

The subject selected for this session at Cranbrook implies a point of view both in the grouping and the order of three terms: history, theory, and criticism. The committee felt a pressing need to reconsider in a new light the sources of humanizing potentials for architecture in our era when the pervasive influence of science with all its automated technology tends to make lessons from the past seem irrelevant.

In spite of increased attention that deans of schools and many progressive architects have given to history as a *cultural* subject, there is little evidence to show that either the schools in general or the profession understand or creatively use the historical study of architecture within its time context. Many still view the study of history suspiciously as a negative obsession rather than as a positive force in determining the present and future course of both education and architecture. The frequent and gratuitous identification of history with eclecticism exposes a point of view that now should be obsolete among architects; it overlooks newer methods and interpretations of historical examples which for many years have been fundamental to the work of avant-garde leaders. The papers in this volume argue the merits of various approaches, but the need to search is implicit in them all.

Perhaps, because so many architects would rather draw than read, history is still static to those who first saw it that way when, as students, they slept through slide lectures that were more concerned with *what* than *why*. Since then, many have traveled sufficiently among historical settings to awaken an intuitive response; but few have taken the time to discover the potential dynamic relationship between theory and criticism of modern architecture and its evolving past. One explanation of the prevalent "modern eclecticism" and the pursuit of ephemeral fashions in design may be found in lack of a solid basis for working theory—a basis that creative architects could derive from recent experience and support by the intelligent use of historical knowledge and scientific critical method. Until architects, by their works, demonstrate an understanding of history to the American public, we may continue to witness the vulgarized parodies of reconstructed Williamsburg spread like tumbleweed from one end of the country to another.

In selecting the theme for the 1964 seminar, the committee hoped to focus some attention on the need in the schools of architecture and in the profession to place a new emphasis upon the ecological aspect of historical buildings and spaces in American cities as well as those in older cultures. Lacking the slower pace of the earlier times which enabled our ancestors to sift, sample, test, and either reject or absorb the vital ideas contributed by the most creative architects and critics, we dash from one set of fashionable innovations to another leaving unexplored the potentials of our recent past along the way. In our haste to be avant-garde, we lose any useful continuity with the best of our own traditions. We may feel but cannot effectively explain the significance of native environment in design terms. Too often we are embarrassed when confronted with problems of preservation and the compatibility of modern buildings with older ones. After a hundred years of architectural education in this country we still try to acquire architectural values vicariously from those who, we believe, have roots in *their own* traditions. The implications of this historical fact remain to be seriously examined by both ACSA and AIA.

The authors of the seminar papers are all distinguished teachers or critics, architecturally *engagé*; their contributions were intended primarily to stimulate discussion at the Cranbrook sessions. Although their perceptive comments and arguments were especially prepared to be delivered in person, the edited results can also be read as a collection of provocative essays, which will interest a much larger audience. The participants at Cranbrook found a minimum of ashes amidst this volume of live coals: fuel easily fanned to flame. A thoughtful review of these papers is recommended especially to the faculties of each school of architecture and to the program planners of each chapter of AIA. The challenge for action is clear.

Washington University, St. Louis
December, 1964

AIA-ACSA TEACHER SEMINAR 1964

Steering Committee

LAWRENCE B. ANDERSON, *General Chairman*
DONALD Q. FARAGHER, *Finances*
HENRY L. KAMPHOEFNER

Scholarship Committee

HENRY L. KAMPHOEFNER, *Chairman*
HENRY A. MILLON
KAREL YASKO
MAURICE W. PERREAULT

Program Committee

HENRY A. MILLON, *Chairman*
BUFORD L. PICKENS, *Moderator*
PETER COLLINS
WALTER L. CREESE
THOMAS HOWARTH
ROBERT H. SNYDER
MAURICE W. PERREAULT, *Staff*
MARCUS WHIFFEN, *Editor*
JO ANN CHATELAIN, *Project Associate*

CONTENTS

ILLUSTRATION

The History, Theory
and Criticism of
Architecture

THE INTERRELATED ROLES OF HISTORY, THEORY, AND CRITICISM IN THE PROCESS OF ARCHITECTURAL DESIGN

Peter Collins

The topic which concerns us here today would have been inconceivable before 1750. The history of architecture, as we understand it, was not thought of as an academic professional discipline until the middle of the eighteenth century; hence the theory of architecture was virtually unaffected by broadly-based historical scholarship. Similarly, though judgment on the merits and defects of buildings is, in some form or another, presumably as old as architecture itself, modern architectural criticism cannot, to my knowledge, be traced back before 1751, when Jacques-François Blondel published his *Architecture Françoise* for the students of his newly founded school of architecture (the first full-time school of architecture to exist). The most urgent tasks before us today, then, would seem to me to be (a) an evaluation of the ideal relationship between architectural theory and architectural history, and (b) an evaluation of the influence which the study of architectural history should have on architectural criticism, considered as an aspect of design.

First, then, let us consider our modern attitude towards the history of architecture. The first dilemma which confronts anyone dealing with this subject's place in an architectural curriculum is: "Should the history of architecture be taught at all?" One can argue convincingly that many great buildings were constructed before any text-books on the history of architecture were written, and that it was the emergence of text-books on the history of architecture which produced Revivalism—a phenomenon which many teachers of architecture regard as a fundamental defect without any redeeming qualities. One can also argue that the reaction against Revivalism in the first quarter of the present century was only accomplished initially by banning lectures on the history of architecture from architectural curricula; for although Walter Gropius sufficiently modified his views after his arrival at Harvard to admit courses in architectural

1

history, they had been rigorously banned from the Bauhaus. Moreover, he only propagated his new liberal attitude with the proviso that such courses should be given to students sufficiently advanced and mature to have found their self-expression—i.e., who had already evolved their own philosophy of architectural design. Gropius therefore presumably argued that the study of the history of architecture makes no contribution towards the evolution of a contemporary theory of architecture, and that it may even militate against it; for he asserted that "when the innocent beginner is introduced to the great achievements of the past, he may too easily be discouraged from trying to create for himself."

This matter will doubtless be dealt with thoroughly on Thursday, but if I may here interpolate my own views on Gropius' attitude, without irrelevance or irreverence, I believe that it is impossible, even if it were desirable, to keep an architectural student totally ignorant of architectural history. Thus the task of those who administer schools of architecture should not be to immunize new students against the evils of architectural historicism by prophylactic isolation, but to inoculate them with carefully measured doses, in such a way that new students become, as it were, vaccinated against epidemics of historicism whilst at the same time obtaining the basic ideas on which to evolve a theory of design.

However, there are many teachers who, whilst bearing no hostility towards the teaching of architectural history, consider that it makes no contribution towards the formation of an architectural philosophy and merely plays the same cultural role in the formation of a student's character as social and political history plays in forming the character of a graduate in the liberal arts. I do not intend to examine here the merits and defects of this argument, since they also can appropriately be relegated for discussion on Thursday. There is however one implication of the point of view I should like to formulate for your consideration now, namely: If the study of the history of architecture *is* a means towards obtaining a theory of architecture, does it matter whether those who teach the history of architecture to architectural students are trained architects or not? In other words, should we argue that no one is qualified to teach the history of architecture to architectural students unless he has had some personal experience of designing buildings?

The third dilemmna in considering the place of the history of architecture in an architectural curriculum concerns the relationship of architecture to the other arts. If architecture is considered to be simply what Vasari called one of the 'arts of design', then clearly the history of architecture must be considered to be of the same character as the history of painting, the history of sculpture, the history of jewelry, and the history of every other artifact. Indeed, according to Gropius, "the term 'design' broadly embraces the whole orbit of man-made visible surroundings, from simple everyday goods to the whole complex pattern of a whole town . . . and the process of designing a great building or a simple chair differs only in degree, not in principle."

It is important to realize that this is essentially an Italian Renaissance theory of architecture, and Vasari's *Lives of the Painters, Sculptors and Architects* is to this extent based on the same philosophy as Gropius' *The New Architecture and the Bauhaus*. I mention this because it was the French seventeenth and eighteenth century architects' refusal to regard themselves as affiliated with painters and sculptors which constituted the principal bulwark of the Rationalist doctrine with which the Bauhaus is so often identified. It will therefore be quite apparent that one's views on this particular topic will fundamentally affect one's opinion regarding the way the history of architecture should be taught, if it is taught at all.

Having now indicated what seem to me to be the three main attitudes one can take towards the teaching of architectural history in schools of architecture, I should like to suggest some of the ways that the history of architecture can be taught to architectural students by teachers who believe that the history of architecture is an important source of every architect's theory of architecture. This clearly assumes that there *is* such a thing as 'the theory of architecture'—a notion strenuously repudiated by such an authority as Professor Lord Llewellyn-Davies. If, however, I may be allowed to assume, for the sake of my present argument, that there is such a thing as the theory of architecture; and if I may be allowed (pending tomorrow's discussion) to define it roughly as the principles which relate the form of a building to the sociological, technological, economic and aesthetic conditions presiding over its inception, I think I may say that this theory of architecture can be deduced by three means, two of which are dependent on architectural history and the third on its self-conscious rejection.

We are all familiar with the rejection of architectural history by those theorists who believe that "pure form" can be created by "pure thought" based simply on current sociology, current psychology and current theories of structure. Similarly, we are all familiar with the notion that a theory of architecture can be based on "contemporary practice" (by which is usually meant the buildings publicized by architectural magazines in the last few years). I would hazard a guess, however, that most architects reject the view—so innocently adopted twenty-five years ago by those seeking to figure as leaders of the profession—that good buildings can be designed in a historical vacuum. Not only do they believe in a theory of architecture, but they believe that such a theory should result from the considered analysis of buildings constructed in many different centuries, many different latitudes, and many different social conditions. I believe that one of our most important tasks in this seminar is to decide what limitations, if any, the study of architectural history should have.

To begin, then, with the problem of chronology: When does the history of architecture begin and when does it end? Most people, I imagine, would share Professor Millon's view that it begins about 3500 B.C. and ends with the latest building by Skidmore, Owings and Merrill. I would suggest, however, that if the history of architecture is to be thought of as primarily the source of the theory of architecture, it should be considered as ending at least a decade before the present, and as beginning at an age really classified as history, and not as pre-history.[1]

---

[1] Certain views put forward by some members of the audience indicated, in the subsequent discussion, that my attitude towards pre-history was misunderstood. I am of course well aware that all buildings, however chronologically primitive, can be regarded as "historical." But to historians concerned with the general cultural past of mankind, there is a very clear distinction between buildings built in historical ages (i.e., by societies which have bequeathed us ample written records) and those built in pre-historic ages (i.e., by societies virtually unknown apart from what can be deduced from their few surviving artefacts). If one believes, as I do, that it is important to have a broad independent factual knowledge of the main conditions of the *program* before assessing buildings and discussing architectural ideas, it will be apparent why I consider a study of the buildings of "historical" ages more rewarding for architectural students than the study of buildings of "pre-historic" ages.

As regards the terminal date, we are too much a part of the 1950's and 1960's to make dispassionate judgments on the historical value of buildings constructed in our own day; and if anyone here doubts this, let him reflect on the importance he now attaches to the new buildings he admired when he was a student. As regards the initial date, we are intellectually, emotionally and financially too remote from the stone age to draw useful conclusions from the way they then arranged their megaliths. Similarly, though I am willing to admit that fascinating parallels can be drawn between Assyrian Ziggurats and the Guggenheim museum, I myself consider it more useful, in the time available, to begin with Greek temples and to end at about 1950. However the precise dates are a matter of personal convenience. What matters is whether or not we deliberately organize our history courses to provide the basis of speculation about architectural theory, because if we do, we shall certainly evolve a chronological and geographical equilibrium very different from that which suits architectural history considered as simply a cultural exercise.

As regards the problem of geographical distribution, most teachers of architectural history would frown upon any deliberate policy imposing geographical limitations, even though time-tables undoubtedly necessitate restrictions and omissions of some kind. So anxious are many teachers to demonstrate their lack of prejudice in this respect that they go out of their way to deal with out-of-the-way examples, occasionally finishing up with the kind of exoticism they would be the first to reprove with respect to the nineteenth century. I hope there will be some opportunity to discuss exoticism in relation to history and theory. I myself virtually ignore Chinese, Japanese, and Indian architecture, though I feel sure there are many here who would claim that North American civilization has more affinity with, say, Japanese culture than with European culture. Doubtless some of you would argue that modern frame construction has more affinity with traditional Japanese frame construction than with traditional European frame construction. Even so, I would still argue that the expression Western Civilization imposes certain obligations on our teaching here which correspond to a very real quality in our culture; for as the Japanese Ambassador to Canada once wittily remarked, one soon becomes aware in

North America that the East is to the west and the West is
to the east.

At this point, it will, I think, be opportune to consider the
relationship between architectural history and architectural criticism. For many professional architectural historians, criticism
involves what are sometimes disparagingly called "value judgments", and these are thought of as in some way inimical to true
scholarship. However, as James Ackerman points out in his book
Art and Archaeology, the isolation of art history from art criticism in recent times is due largely to an unjustifiable conviction
that a clear distinction can be made between facts and feelings
about works of art, whereas in fact such a distinction does not
exist. There are, I suspect, few lecturers in architectural history
who *do* achieve absolutely dispassionate objectivity, even though
their subjectivity may consist only in keeping silent about buildings which they do not consider well designed.

As an example of what I mean, let us take a famous monument of the Age of Louis XIV: the great stables of Versailles.
Now Jacques-François Blondel (a practicing architect as well
as one of the greatest teachers who has ever lived) remarked in
his history lectures delivered in 1750 that these stables were
among the three finest buildings in France erected in the second
half of the seventeenth century. In contrast, the ten best known
general histories of architecture written in the English language
do not even mention these stables, though many of these text-
books include such recondite examples as Asiatic rock-cut tombs,
carvings which I myself do not consider to be architecture at all.

Let us assume, however, that by criticism we do not simply
mean the omission of buildings thought to deserve censure, but
positive statements of a point of view, both for and against.
The sort of thing I have in mind can be exemplified effectively
by reference again to the great stables at Versailles, this time
by quoting Reginald Blomfield's remarks upon them in his
thorough monograph on French architecture built between 1661
and 1774. "The entrance front of the Grande Ecurie," he
writes, "is one of the most satisfactory pieces of architecture at
Versailles. The central doorway is rather clumsy, and the trophies below the string-course are too low on the piers; indeed
they might have been omitted with advantage to the design,
but the scale is well maintained, and the planes are very well

managed." If this is what you will agree to call architectural criticism, then it would seem that it can be exercised in three possible ways: firstly, by reference to the lecturer's personal emotions; secondly, by reference to formulated principles (especially to principles formulated or known in the era the building was constructed); and thirdly, by reference to fashions accepted in the age in which we now live.

Criticism by reference to personal emotions is best exemplified, to my knowledge, by the technique of Vincent Scully, and in case anyone should think that this remark is intended as a sneer, I hasten to say immediately that I consider Scully to be one of the greatest living architectural historians. No one is better qualified to lecture on architecture to the layman; however, we are not concerned in this seminar with lectures given to laymen but with lectures given to architectural students, and in this respect I would suggest that whilst Scully is one of the finest promoters of architectural sensitivity among the lay intelligentsia, his lectures suffer from the same defect as those of John Ruskin; namely, they are over-concerned with translating poetic emotions into phrases that adequately convey their full poetic quality. In other words, Scully's approach is what Oscar Wilde was writing about in his essay entitled "The Critic as an Artist," and there are many art historians today who hold the same view. However, as I have already indicated, I do not believe architectural history to be simply a branch of art history, and even if I did, I would not believe that architectural criticism should be judged as if it were blank verse.

The second kind of criticism, namely criticism by reference to formulated principles, can be of two types. Either it can mean criticism by reference to principles evolved by the lecturer or it can mean criticism by reference to principles formulated by someone else. Personally, I see nothing ignominious in accepting another person's theory of architecture—however long ago it was formulated—provided one does not accept it blindly and mechanically, but assents to it only after a lengthy period of intellectual search. Moreover, I see no reason to believe that lecturing in accordance with specific and uncompromising principles implies dictatorially thrusting a doctrine upon each student's impressionable young mind (especially if one regards the history of architecture as the history of the theory of archi-

tecture). The lecturer who describes the theories of earlier architects, and who lectures in accordance with specific principles of
his own, does nothing subversive. He merely asserts to each
student, by his example, that every architect is morally bound
to criticize (and design critically) in accordance with principles,
and there are few students who are so spineless that they accept
their teacher's doctrines without also studying those published
by other teachers, or exemplified by living architects they admire.

Perhaps in the discussion this afternoon, we shall hear over-
riding objections to this point of view, but I would like here to
emphasize one of its great advantages, namely, that it allows
one, better than any other philosophy or system, to base a lecture
course in history on those buildings which are most abundantly
documented. Bruce Allsopp, in his *History of Renaissance Architecture,* remarks that the Palace of Versailles "has something
in common with the unimaginative palaces of Assyrian Kings."
Now whether this remark is true or not, it must be perfectly
apparent that by spending twice as much time on Versailles, and
omitting altogether the palace at Khorsabad, one can teach
architectural students far more useful ideas about the principles
(i.e. the theory) on which judgment should be based. For our
knowledge of Assyrian technology, Assyrian social conditions,
Assyrian economic conditions, and Assyrian political conditions
is negligible compared with our knowledge of those which
existed in the age of Louis XIV. Moreover, and most important
of all, the palace of Versailles still has a roof on it, whereas the
palace at Khorsabad does not even have the walls to support
one. One could also add that not only is the palace of Versailles
structurally complete, but many of the preliminary drawings,
later codified or abandoned, have been preserved.

I know that it is now popular for art historians who write
about modern architecture to show triumphantly that there are
affinities between the plans of Louis Kahn, Gerhard Kallmann
or other avant-garde architects and the excavated ruins of
ancient Crete; but this is simply an example of the popular
art-historical game of "hunt the precedent." If the new city hall
at Boston is in fact modeled on restorations based upon the
cellars at Knossos, then it is presumably an example of the
Formalism so popular in the nineteenth century, which is now
so popularly condemned. But Boston city hall is not yet, I

would contend, a part of architectural history, whilst the palace at Knossos is so fragmentary and poorly documented that, for architectural students, it deserves only passing mention.

There would seem little need for me to discuss criticism based on fashion, since its dangers are obvious to everyone. Nevertheless, I hope that this topic will be dealt with in this afternoon's discussion, for it is the aspect of the relationship between architectural history, architectural theory and architectural criticism which I find least easy to resolve. It is easy to be priggish and aloof, and to interpret history or assess new buildings without regard for popular opinion. It is easy to make a fetish of modernism, and make sure that everything one writes or says is in harmony with current notions of being avant-garde. The difficulty is to strike an honorable mean between the two, whilst at the same time retaining the respect of one's students; for the mind of youth is in this domain particularly difficult to fathom.

HISTORY AS A METHOD OF
TEACHING ARCHITECTURE

Bruno Zevi

The conclusions of this seminar are not going to remain Platonic. We shall try to apply them in our schools, starting with the Facoltà di Architettura of the University of Rome, where for the past year I have occupied the chair of architectural history.

Let me tell you something about my school. The Facoltà di Architettura at Rome is not very important, but the influence of Rome is still relevant. The school is housed in a lousy building up on the hill of Valle Giulia, in a sector of the city where the majority of the foreign academies are located. If it were a good school, if it were to be renewed according to the principles that we shall work out here at Cranbrook, it could carry weight in the architectural world.

Well, what is the story of this school? Briefly, it was first reactionary, then Fascist, and finally "empirical," so to speak. It started in 1921 on academical lines; during the Mussolini period it went "monumental" in the most vulgar meaning of the word. Then, after the last war, it adopted the sort of attitude that many architectural schools have; courses were multiplied, a lot of people were invited to visit the school, a terrific number of things were done without any unifying thought, all in the belief that when you don't have an idea you can conceal the fact just by multiplying the instruments. But in Rome this system did not work. Last year, the students occupied the school for forty-two days and nights—forty-two! It is a long time—simply in reaction against it. Under the pressure of this occupation, which brought about a one-day strike of the whole university, new professors were called to Rome—one to fill the town-planning chair, the second to fill the design chair, the third to fill the history of architecture chair.

We started to remake the school. We made a plan for its transformation. The battle lasted almost an entire year, from November, when I entered the school, until last Wednesday.

Only last Wednesday, the faculty council (that is the council of the full professors) approved a motion which said that *the teaching of architecture should be based on the historical method*. Actually in Italian it says *metodo storico-critico* because there is no history without criticism.

Here we come immediately to the central problem of this seminar. Let us recognize right away that our problem is not how to teach history of architecture, theory of architecture or architectural criticism but *how to teach architecture*. That is what our schools are for, and we have to find out how to teach architecture with a method that is less empirical, less approximate than those adopted up to now.

How has architecture been taught up to now? I am not going to give you a history of architectural education. However, we can say that three methods have been employed. The first, starting with the Renaissance, was the *bottega* method. A young man who wanted to be an architect would select a master, would go to work and learn in his *bottega* or office. In all the schools where you have few students and a great personality among the teachers, this method still continues. Is it good? Perhaps it *was* good, but it does not work any more. It is the typical method of the *élite* school, while we have to face the problem of mass-education. I remember that when I was at Harvard, Gropius had about twelve students in his master course, and he used to say that they were too many, that he couldn't follow twelve students. In Rome, in the five-year course, we have 2,500 students. Perhaps you can divide the school into two or into three, but you are not going to solve the problem, which today is mass-education as against *élite*-education.

There is another drawback in this method. To follow a master is not really a guarantee that you are going to get his process, and not merely his results. We have seen people who have been for years at Taliesin or in Mies van der Rohe's school, and very often they did not get the process at all. They got the results; they became little Wrights, little Mieses.

And then where are the masters, where are the great personalities today? Around 1940 an American boy could select his master more or less as a boy of the Renaissance could select a master among many important painters. You could go to Harvard if you liked Gropius, you could go to Chicago to follow

Mies, you could select Wright and go to Taliesin. But this "heroic" period of modern architecture is coming to an end. It looks as if the new generation is not producing heroes, perhaps because we are not asking for them anymore, because the hero-system of teaching architecture is by now rather obsolete. We are looking for a scientific method.

As for the second system of the past—you know it only too well. It is the academic system, the Beaux-Arts. History was taught as "styles," phenomena were reduced to rules. Design teaching was also directed towards a style, and so it could easily meet history. Out of the meeting between this kind of history and this kind of design teaching the theory of architecture was formulated with its idols of proportion, symmetry, dynamic composition, rhythm and so on. The theory made the school perfectly coherent, with the perfection of a tomb. It resulted in the death of history, and the death of original creativity. I said that it resulted in them. But it would be better to say frankly that it results in them, because many of our schools are still run on the Beaux-Arts system, only with less coherence.

The modern movement in architecture produced a crisis in this system. And at this point we have a big episode, one that is well known but should be constantly present during our discussions because it is the most significant and dramatic fact of the last decades. I refer to the Bauhaus.

In the Bauhaus we find a marriage between the modern movement in architecture and modern pedagogy. That is, people were to learn not by listening to lectures from the professor, but by doing things themselves. Learning became an active proposition. But what about the teaching of history? As you know, Gropius threw it out of the Bauhaus curriculum. Why? With a few exceptions—and perhaps those were not available in Weimar and Dessau—the architectural historians were all more or less reactionary. They thought that architectural history stopped at the end of the eighteenth century. They conceived historical phenomena as "styles" and therefore, if they had to include the modern movement in their history courses, they would simply add one more style to the variety of the past. This was the traditional, Beaux-Arts, reactionary way of interpreting history, and Gropius was fully justified in rejecting it. But he made a mistake. Instead of stating that he could not have history courses because there were no good modern historians around, he constructed a funny theory according to which history, especially at the beginning, would have a negative influence on the architectural student, would influence him too much, would paralyze his creative impulse. This was the tragedy. It meant the failure not only of historical and critical teaching, but also of the possibility of finding a modern method of teaching architecture. The baby was thrown out with the bath-water. Given the fact that there was nobody around to teach history of architecture in a modern way, instead of trying to stimulate young historians they decided not to teach history. So you had, on one hand, the past left to the reactionary historians; on the other, the modern movement with no historical perspective—that is, up in the air. No integration, no history, old styles on one side, the modern "style" on the other. The new pedagogy had no influence on the history courses.

Here is the drama. From the time of the Bauhaus until this seminar at Cranbrook, nothing has been done to overcome the gap, the gulf between the teaching of history and the teaching of design. You will agree that our schools are going on without a real untiy of approach: we have design courses, based on empirical methods, and we have history courses which remain academical no matter who is teaching. Sure, I know, we are all excellent teachers of history, fully permeated by the modern movement and by the modern art criticism. Our classes are crowded with students. They listen to our lectures with enthusiasm, because we open to them big panoramas; we are able to show that even a Greek temple, even a Roman basilica or a Baroque church is a "modern" building if you see it with modern eyes, if you "read" it with a contemporary spirit.

This is all very well. But the effect of our courses on the drafting-boards is practically non-existent. The gap is still there. A good history professor will have, no doubt, a positive influence on the cultural atmosphere of the school, but his direct impact on the method of producing architecture is still very small. Given the fact that you cannot have a coherent school of architecture unless you reach a real integration between history and design, we have reached the nadir.

In the meantime we have more and more schools. Everybody is looking for teachers, chairmen, deans. In Italy, at least twice a year we receive an invitation to come to the United States to head some important American school of architecture. You cannot expect to find big personalities to lead all the new schools of architecture of the world. And then, as we have seen, the *bottega*, the hero-system is dated by now. We must find a new method, which you can apply even with average teachers, just as you could apply the Beaux-Arts system wherever you wanted.

For a whole year in Rome we have been discussing a third system of teaching architecture, a system based on the historical method, and therefore totally different from both the *bottega* and the Beaux-Arts systems. It is the fascinating hypothesis of a new school of architecture, of a Bauhaus pregnant, so to speak, with historical—that is to say, scientific—consciousness.

In order to explain this hypothesis, we have to consider some of the basic premises of the contemporary philosophy of art. If we are going to build new schools of architecture, we have, first of all, to be in line with modern aesthetics. There are at least three basic concepts that we should always keep in mind.

First, we should remember that the idea that art is something purely intuitive, irrational, something that has to do only with feelings, is outdated. Art is a conscious act, a process which can be controlled and verified throughout. You can teach the process in a scientific way with the methods of modern scientific research, which are not static and mechanical but give ample scope to hypothesis, to the unknown, to the creative spirit.

Secondly, there is the consideration that so-called works of art are not always of a creative nature. In point of fact, a great many works of art, even very famous works of art, are of a critical nature. You can use words to write a poem, or just to tell a story, or to criticize an event. It is the same with painting. You can sing and you can speak. Modern art criticism has been able to show that many painters were really not artists but critics, great critics who used the medium of painting instead of the medium of words to express not their feelings but their ideas. And it is the same with architecture. In the best cases, our students will be good critics who will express their ideas in architecture, through building. The creative genius is rather rare in any century, and schools are not for geniuses, or at least not for them alone.

Thirdly, we should recognize that in the very few, exceptional works of art that are creative, there is a process that we can grasp and demonstrate and verify, just behind the lyrical or poetic aspect which appears irrational. A few years ago, we had a most interesting debate about Dante in Italy. It was obvious that Dante was a poet, but it was equally evident that the *Divine Comedy* was not made up only of poetry; it has a logical, planned, conscious structure. Could the two things be divided? A great Italian philosopher, Benedetto Croce, tried. He wrote a book entitled *Poetry and Non-Poetry in Dante*, in which he separated the verses which could be considered true poetry from those which were clearly the expression of conscious thought. Well, this method of analysis did not work. You could make an anthology of poetical passages of the *Divine Comedy* but, in doing so, you would kill the *Divine Comedy*. One cannot separate, even in the greatest creation, what is lyrical from what is not. They are indissolubly fused. You cannot understand the creative parts of the *Divine Comedy* without considering, at the same time, its critical parts. The irrational and the rational are dependent upon each other.

From these three basic discoveries of modern aesthetics came modern historical research. The method consists of entering into the work of art, of reconstructing the process of its making in order to understand why the artist does what he does and not something different, and especially to understand how he corrects himself and why. The most revealing studies of poetry are those which examine the corrections the poet made in his various manuscripts. Here he is substituting one word, there another. Why? In every case, you can demonstrate the reason, what he is changing, why he is putting in something that was not there before. With architectural sketches, it is the same thing; you can use the method with drawings by Michelangelo or sketches by Frank Lloyd Wright, and you can grasp every phase, almost every moment of their creative process.

Well, here we are at Cranbrook, not to find out how to teach history of architecture—for in six days it is doubtful whether you can learn how to become a good historian if you are not one already—but to find out how, being excellent historians, we can contribute to the building of good schools of architecture. We know that the hero-system of teaching is finished. We know that the Beaux-Arts system is outdated. We know, out of the Bauhaus experience, that design teaching has to meet modern pedagogy. And finally we know that history courses, in our schools, when they are well done, arouse the enthusiasm more than any other course, in spite of the fact that they have little relevance on the drafting boards. Our problem therefore is difficult but, at least, clear. We have to find a system of teaching design with a historical method, so as to achieve a complete coherence, almost a fusion between history courses and design courses—a cultural integration such as we had in the Beaux-Arts, only the other way around, of a modern, dynamic, open, scientific kind. That is what we have to achieve. How?

Let us consider, for a moment, our history courses. We have rejected the idea of "styles," that is of history as something static and dogmatic. We are able to show to the students that every great monument of the past is "modern." We make no distinction between history, theory and criticism because we know that you cannot have history without a theoretical approach and without critical involvement. Finally, we know that history is an active process, as it is concerned with the identification of the dynamic process through which a work of art comes to life. There is no longer any gulf between history teaching and modern pedagogy, no longer war between history and the modern movement. If Gropius had to organize a Bauhaus today, would he admit history courses?

I believe that he would, or at least that the contents of our courses and our intentions would incline him to do so. But the instruments we use might make him hesitate. Our instruments are obsolete. We are trying to do a modern history with the old instruments, writing and speaking. The real obstacle we meet in our attempt to teach architecture by a historical method derives from the fact that we are teaching history with only words. Words are not the means the architect uses for his work, and the challenge for us, in the next few years, will be to find a method by which historical research can be done with the architect's instruments. Now, we know that a critical essay can be produced by painting, as in the case of the Carracci, as in the case of the great majority of modern painters. Is there any reason why the same could not be done in architecture? Why not express architectural criticism in architectural forms instead of in words? Is it impossible? In Italy we are starting to experiment. We are still at the very beginning of this kind of research, but the way we are following is the right one.

When I was teaching at Venice, until last year, we tried to invent this new kind of criticism—architectural criticism expressed with architectural instruments. We concentrated on Michelangelo's architecture, in view of the celebrations of this year. Every time we had a critical thought to express, a real idea about Michelangelo, we tried to manifest it three-dimensionally. The results of this work, done over three years by the students at Venice, can be seen in the great Michelangelo exhibition in Rome, at the Palazzo delle Esposizioni in Via Nazionale. Some photographs of the critical models we prepared can be seen in the January 1964 issue of my magazine *L'architettura: cronache e storia*. We are far from satisfied with this experiment, but I think that it is valuable insofar as it demonstrates that architectural criticism or architectural history can be "written" in another way than with words.

If the experiment is carried on, perhaps our goal of an integrated architectural culture, and therefore of a good, modern school of architecture, is not too far off. If history uses the instruments of design, the reverse is also true: Design is going to use the instruments of history and criticism more and more. What the students of our schools resent more than anything else is the superficial, empirical, anti-scientific way in which their designs are criticized. How does the design critic express himself? Too often in the vaguest way: "Rather nice. A bit weak here; perhaps you could put more tension on this side. Why don't you make this part of the building more fluent?"—all that kind of baloney. We have thrown out the old, academical grammar and syntax, but having failed to replace them with new grammars and new syntaxes, open and dynamic, we find ourselves empty-handed. At this point, however, the new historical method comes to the help of the design courses, just as design methods come to the help of history. If history is now able to reconstruct the creative processes of the builder of a Gothic cathedral, or of Brunelleschi, or Bramante, or Wren, it is also able to follow, to control and to test the process of architectural creation. The method for understanding an old building and for criticizing a new one in the very process of creation is the

same. If design criticism at the drafting-tables is going to become scientific, it must adopt the historical method in the new,
active, operative sense which has been underlined. Otherwise,
design critics will continue to be prima-donnas expressing, with
poor words, their feelings merely. The good design critic today,
with the new science at his disposal, cannot but be a historian,
just as the good historian is the one man who can understand
and verify the inner process of a design. Design, in fact, is
going to be taught in the history courses or (better) in the
history laboratory; and history is going to be taught at the
drafting-tables. This is the challenge for all of us. We have to
merge history and design courses, renewing the methods of both.

If we are able to achieve this goal, we shall not only have a
school as coherent as the Beaux-Arts (upside-down); we shall
also keep what is good in the *bottega* method of teaching, putting it at the disposal of mass-education.

What I mean is this. Many masters are dead; a student cannot go to their offices. The masters who are alive can accept
only a few students in their offices, and they don't have the
time or the will to explain their processes. But the new historical
method can explain them. We can teach Wright better than
Wright. We can teach Le Corbusier better than he could. We
can explain the break from the Villa Savoye to Ronchamp,
while Le Corbusier, in homage to the myth of coherence, would
deny that there is a break. In other words, merging history and
design, renewing history with the dynamic design approach, and
design with the new historical method, we can achieve an integrated culture, and have a school for the masses without re-
nouncing the benefits of the *bottega* and of the Beaux-Arts.

I could stop right here. Indeed, I have spoken much too
much. But if you have invited me to come from Italy to Cranbrook, it must be because you want to know everything I know.
In fact, I don't know much more than I have said; I put in
front of you problems, not solutions. I am here to learn, and to
have you judge what we are trying to do in Rome.

Let me conclude by referring to the questionnaire that was
sent to all the speakers at this seminar. Among other things it
asked: Is contemporary architecture a legitimate subject of
historical research? A most incredible question! It is obvious
that, without historical research, we are going to waste the

heritage of the modern movement, to continue to rediscover modern architecture every morning, to play at being the vanguard instead of creating an architectural language for modern architecture's maturity. I can give you an example of the state of our knowledge where the modern movement is concerned. Two weeks ago I was in Florence for the Maggio Musicale Fiorentino, which is dedicated this year to Expressionism. The musician Roman Vlad had decided to perform the opera *The Nose* by Dimitri Shostakovich, which was written in 1928. It was not an easy task. Believe it or not, neither the music nor the words of this opera written in 1928 could be found. Roman Vlad found an act in Moscow, but only one. Then he heard that somebody might have another act in Vienna, and he was lucky enough to find it. But some parts were still missing, and the Communist party had to put political pressure on the Soviet Union to get them to dig them out. No archaeological research is so difficult. The documents of our own time are dispersed or destroyed, especially those concerning Expressionism. The conspiracy against Expressionism started before Hitler and continued after Hitler. In Expressionism Germany was looking at herself in the mirror. Very few people liked this image before Nazism, and very few after. Even now, Germany prefers not to look in the mirror, but to accept a neo-International Style tendency in a neo-capitalist American version. Brecht? Sure, something you can admire and put in the archives . . . Mind you, it is an international conspiracy as was proved at the symposium "Architecture 1918-1928: from the Novembergruppe to the CIAM," organized by the Department of Art History and Archaeology of Columbia University in May 1962, for at that too everybody tried to run down Expressionism. Among architects, I mean professional architects, ignorance is supreme. After the crisis of the so-called International Style, they are going back to plasticism, doing experiments which are infinitely less courageous and valuable than those done more than forty years ago by the Expressionists. Modern architecture, in this respect, is going back, not forward.

What is happening in Europe is happening also, I am afraid, in the United States. Here we see the dilapidation of the Chicago School buildings, and the dilapidation of the heritage of Frank Lloyd Wright. What's wrong with us? It is historical consciousness that is lacking in our culture, and therefore lacking in our teaching of architecture. I don't know which is the cause and which is the effect. It is not important. Our duty is to struggle at one and the same time for an integrated culture and for a scientific method of teaching architecture.

RANDOM THOUGHTS ON THE ARCHITECTURAL CONDITION

Serge Chermayeff

The distinguished chairman has kindly left out that I am an apostate in this company. I don't like much what you do, I don't like very much *how* you do it, and I don't believe what you are doing serves any good.

There are things which perturb me about this particular meeting: the thing which first shook me was your bibliographical list, a document which, I would say, is loaded. I think it has such singular omissions; conspicuously, the weak documentation of our present times and dilemmas. I cannot understand, for instance, how, Mr. Collins notwithstanding, one can omit from required readings for your professed purposes Mr. Greenough, who by the way first said, "Form follows Function," and not Mr. Sullivan who merely repeated it. Mr. Sullivan's own *Kindergarten Chats* I find more refreshing than anything you list; Mr. Wright, in spite of his egocentricity had great principles to announce. Where are the writings of some of our contemporary prophets such as Le Corbusier, Giedion and the documents of CIAM, and lastly Buckminster Fuller, at the moment when the International Union of Architects has adopted his proposals for a world-wide inventory of resources with which designers will in fact have to work? Not the things they *imagine* they are going to have to work with but the *actual* things they are going to have to work with. The first two volumes can be obtained from Southern Illinois University and I recommend these to you, and any which may follow from this source: a great deal of very useful data of which we are so happily, or shall we say innocently, unaware.

And lastly, of course, I am deeply shocked not to find my own book on the list, which I obviously also recommend strongly, as well as another discussing on a very high level the theory of form: *Some Notes on the Synthesis of Form*, a Ph.D dissertation, just recently published by Harvard, by Christopher Alexander who was my collaborator on the book *Community*

23

and Privacy. Anyhow, it must now be quite clear to you that I
am not of your company because I am obviously not well read
except outside your field, and I commend to those of you who
are young enough to catch up with your reading to become
exactly that.

There is a very great need to study what has been absent
from discussion so far: the larger problems of urbanizing men
in great numbers and great complexity. The word urbanism, or
any substitute for this general notion, has been totally omitted
from discussion so far. I believe this larger expression of architecture in our time deserves priority over single building quality.

For similar reasons I resigned from the AIA some years ago
and have not since had any reason to change my mind. I have
remained in the RIBA, partly out of sentiment of course, partly
because they made me a Fellow, but mainly because they are
extremely serious-minded about the responsibility of architects
who, by definition, are professionals first and foremost.

A professional, as far as I can make out, is somebody who
acts *pro bono publico*—in other words, who has social responsibility and is *not* a business man. I have a quote here which I
am going to read. Mr. William Allen, whom some of you may
have met because he was a visitor all over the place here, is now
the Principal of the Architectural Association in London. He
had this to say after his visit on the occasion of a discussion at
the Royal Institute as to whether they should up their fees.
(The Royal Institute felt that they needed all the money they
could get their hands on to consolidate the position of what is
a weakened profession.)

This is what he says about us: "I was in America about six
months and talked to educators and architects across the United
States and Canada. I became increasingly aware of the tremen-
dous difference between the professions here and in America.
We are all accustomed to look at the glossies and admire the
work of Kahn and others, but when you drop below that level
and talk to architects during ordinary jobs, you find them up
against extraordinary difficulties: terrible fee cutting, fee competition, chiseling of all kinds . . . " In other words, we are
not a profession any longer (those of you who are architects).
Most of you are historians and that is still an honorable profession—but be careful.

He continues: " . . . cities that are terrible investments to the future, for the most part rather horrid places. They do not like public architects over there, they think they are in competition with private practice. The real difference begins to show up when you look at some statistics. Here in England we have fairly good knowledge that we have something like 60% or more of the building industry's total volume of building. The highest figure that anyone could guess at in the States was 30% and the lowest 10%, and the general notion is that it was going down and not up as it is here. This is a very serious state of affairs for American architects, if it is true."

All this is a matter of fact undeniably true, and more and more of the building dollar is spent without any help from architects whatsoever. It is therefore perhaps reasonable at this moment to speculate why this is so.

Mr. Zevi has already told you, and I entirely agree with him, that no matter what you do, how wisely you behave in the classroom, it makes not the slightest difference to the field. The field gets more and more inefficient and vulgar, further away from public purpose. For the world in general terms this means that private appetites for those comforts which are now in the hands of a minority in the Western world, of which we happen to be the chief benefactors, are still unassuaged. If we are going to provide increased and widely distributed comfort, hygiene, health and leisure we had better be very, very careful ourselves because people all over are going to look to us for example. We must not continue on a path of self-destruction. Architects, in particular, must begin to design components of an environment which would be worthy of the aspirations of the rising masses of any country. Uncommon men must learn to serve common man.

I agree with Mr. Zevi unequivocally that although modern architecture has produced some most excellent formal statements and really great inventions, we still have not got one single piece of architecture of total excellence such as the earlier examples in simpler cultures. Of course, new diversity and complexity has something to do with our failure. We have not built anything, for example, which is so admirably designed for contemplation and communion as the great temples, churches and cathedrals of history. The reason for our own failures lies in the program behind the act, the consideration of true purpose, the "why" of building, which has been overlaid by obsolete clichés in a backward-looking culture, so frightened of the future that it finds comfort in imitating the past. We are cowards of the worst kind.

Perhaps Western cultures are on the downgrade because they have little hope, and perhaps the African and Asian people will come up because they are filled with hope. Perhaps they will use art to better effect. I hope so; somebody has to and it doesn't look as if we can. Maybe this is a depressing notion? Actually I am feeling extremely optimistic, personally. I am having the best time of my life being a hermit.

Nevertheless I think the architectural profession, as it is, is obsolete. Much more important, architectural education is in danger of becoming obsolete. For that reason it is always heartening to hear that some great schools which are in very influential positions are about to change radically their methods and attitudes.

The professionals in the field, the practitioners, require continuity of attitude, interest and skill—and they really practice expediency. Their nature is practical and they are in fact conservative. Any deviation or invention in their professions is a very useful piece of public relations or propaganda, providing it doesn't radically depart from the general line. And yet these people who are conservatives are allowed to inspect and accredit the schools of architecture from which, of course, they draw their assistants, and more often than that, as a matter of fact, their so-called inspiration.

Schools are by definition scholarly, exploratory, intellectually adventurous, philosophically long-term minded. Their interest is to deepen and widen the field as a whole, without exaggerated regard for the immediately familiar and practical. Their method is imaginative inquiry. This is true, in relation to architecture in the larger sense of the word, in schools which have planning and other related departments and, of course, more particularly in universities with great extra-departmental facilities and resources. The search for widening and deepening is not only a moral but an intellectual obligation and the student and the teacher and the researcher, in spite of themselves and because of the pressures from the market place, have become in fact opponents of the practitioners.

I am not a historian, as you can obviously see, but I would like to inject an amateur idea which occurred to me as history was being discussed. The practitioner and the academician, until only very recently, could be the same man because each had more or less a common concern. But then the run of the mill building commodity never came under discussion, only the examples of good taste. But the further we go back in history the clearer it becomes that everybody knew what building was about because everybody was involved in the act of building, and in maintenance and reconstruction too; and everybody was absolutely and completely familiar with every purpose of every building put up in the culture in question. This meant that you had continuity of a cultural and technical kind which permitted men to refine that which had been found acceptable, to polish, to achieve superb excellence. Later users gave a *post facto* accolade and the excellent and even the merely good became architecture.

Now, we have no possibility of this kind of gradualism and continuity of either a cultural or technical kind. We must plan instead. Cultures are being politically and technically upset, humanity is being redeployed, the rate of technical change has become the measure of the new world, not its art. If you were to draw a graph of pressures upon contemporary culture this graph would be almost vertical in terms of technical change. Individual biophysical acceptance of this change might show small waves of improvement in health and comfort wherever literacy prevails, in liberalism as exemplified on the American scene of general acceptance of *effects* of technical change, but the graph as a whole would be very flat. The problem obviously is how to close this gap between cause and effect or at the very least prevent it from widening. This is a very important consideration for anybody who wants to teach environmental designers of the future. Environments for whom, for where and for why.

I think it is also characteristic of our early technological era to take technology for granted. Technicians are people who are always with us; they will solve problems. Airplane and automobile rides get precarious and expensive, but of course we can make them "work." As a result there is a general indifference about the true nature of emerging technology, which could become a tool for humanity instead of a menace. As a cover we have now glorified "pure" Art and have made it a remedy for anyone fearful of materialism. We have become ashamed (outside of business) of being thought practical because we have not recognized that technology is a marvellous instrument for the forging of the art of the new future. We try to resuscitate the old future of the nineteenth century, a cozier romantic position. We make eclectic architecture or we "play" with forms of more advanced and sophisticated technology. We are making architecture into sculpture strikingly. One can make anything for effect, and there are always technicians around the corner, "plumbers" who will come and make the thing stand up and work.

We are entering, in spite of all symptoms of unwillingness, an entirely new era about ten years old and Mr. Collins, of course, knows it. A Canadian colleague of his, Marshall McLuhan, summarized this transition best in two marvellous books, which again ought to be on your list, *The Gutenberg Galaxy* and *The Understanding Media*. He suggests that ever since the printed word we have become a visual world. We have been taking the word for the deed because the word is always available. We have much practice in the use of language and linguistic verbalizing. But, as a matter of fact, we are kissing goodbye to this visual, verbal world. Since electronics has become a commonplace and instantaneous audio-visual communication is our tool, together with great mobility, we are entering a "global village" world in which everything is present all the time, on a more complex and more generalized scale, but an equivalent of the old tribal environment which every member of the tribe knew very well, had little incentive or need to talk about but had to see, smell, hear and touch to survive. We are indeed becoming part of a global village and require all necessary sensual and mental awareness to enable man to move freely in an environment which is actual and not merely described.

The differences are so fundamental that as the result of this technical-cultural jump, you historians have to begin to write a new kind of post-history, because that is where we are. Mr. Roderick Seidenberg, an ex-architect, wrote a most interesting book, *The Post-Historic Man,* in which he argues very logically that recently we became as different from historic man as historic man was from pre-historic man, and that we shall become ever more different and that to carry over obsolete habits and monuments for ever is to suffer from an obsession. All this globe-shrinking is of extreme importance.

There is another problem, in this country particularly as Mr. Allen observed: the ubiquitous private practitioner. In architecture there is no public servant, nobody talks much about public service, it is only very recently that the notion, because of the pressures of the time, is emerging at all. Public-oriented planners and designers are now getting into urban renewal offices and city planning offices, staffed no longer by sociologists and economists and demographers exclusively as in the slum clearance era; they are projectors of reconstruction and a total architecture. These anonymous, unknown, usually young architects are operating at a public level and close to decision-makers. This is important not only because they are doing an important task but because they are involved in expenditures which would make even SOM jealous. One city, like Chicago, could spend in one year everything that SOM was responsible for in decades; so they are not doing badly as pioneers. A new activity is emerging, apart from the private practitioner and on a new scale—a very significant change.

Under all these pressures the private practitioner runs the risk of losing his integrity. All that star-making which makes *Time* magazine covers is part and parcel of the prevailing hucksterism of our system. Architects are not only subject to being exploited by the professional hucksters but they themselves are becoming hucksters.

I have a feeling that what has really been happening is that architects have completely missed a position among decision makers. They are worse than hucksters; architects really are hustlers, they are the second oldest profession today, standing on street corners waiting to be picked up, and they think it is a good thing to be picked up by people with a lot of money.

I am sick indeed of expensive scenery. Mr. Zevi, walking around with me yesterday, observed that the scenery close by, the great portico which splits the world of pretty fountains from the world of the water tower, is just waiting to be taken down. It looks exactly like a theatrical set, you just turn off the lights, you knock down the flats and you take it to the next fair ground. It is just scenery and if you look at it very carefully, it becomes worse and worse and more and more emptily decorative and finally slides down into the slough of purposelessness.

Man is extended and at the same time he is deprived. He has become imprisoned in his own devices, frustrated by his own ambition. He is driven mad by his own noises. He is run over by his own mobility. He is inhibited by his own "education." Every time some bright, but not bright enough administrator or professor thinks that it would be awfully good for architectural students to receive, within a too short time package, another message from another god, it goes into the curriculum.

Our physicists are beginning to learn much more about how to educate, as are also the mathematicians. What happens in architecture? Schools expect the students, in a very short slice of their experience labeled education, to digest many more impressions than in fact it is humanly possible to do. Again for your reading list I suggest you look up various articles by Mr. Richard L. Meier. There is evidence which puts the optimum amount of impressions that may be absorbed simultaneously by the average human being at seven.[1] The permutations of seven are in the millions. This is quite a lot of converting to do. Perhaps what we have to do as educators is not to increase our offerings but to improve quality—not to spread our teaching time thin but to enrich the presentation of what is intended to be conveyed.

I am going to suggest two things which may not be properly taught in the spectrum of time as short as are the formal slices of education dedicated currently to architecture. You may not teach art because that is *post facto* evaluation of work accomplished, and you certainly cannot teach much technology because mostly it becomes obsolete before the chap gets out of school. So what is left to teach? Exactly what everybody has been hinting at and not coming out with: it is principles, a philosophically based process of tackling problems of organization. It is a set of intellectual and ethical rules of behavior and

---

[1] On this see also Edward L. Walker in *The Teaching of Architecture,* edited by Marcus Whiffen. (Washington: American Institute of Architects, 1964), pp. 38-46.—*Editor.*

guidance toward appropriate choice of tools as and when the specific and the particular becomes visible. The artistic act and technical knowledge are quite different from general principles; the two shall not be muddled in the mind. It has taken me, lacking educational help, forty years to separate art from technics and the philosophical principle from the particular case. So maybe some basic revision in the education of future designers is in order.

I mention obsolescence as being a factor in our life, as the reason why we cannot attempt to teach technology in any direct way. But we can certainly discuss natural forces and structural systems which enable us to achieve a growing variety of purposes. We are entering into an entirely new era; we can add to our structural and formal vocabulary an organic equilibrium, living, organic structures of infinitely higher performance than anything which we have previously known. For an architect, it is clearly fascinating to speculate about new purposes and new techniques. We can imagine structures which in fact will live; and we can imagine places which will accommodate new life. Technically most things are already possible and open new architectural vistas. But how few architects are aware of them! Buildings get bigger and more precise and more complex. More and more components of an organic type have to be built into the architectural equation.

As for the cube as a structurally sound container, I owe it to Bucky Fuller that I can only see it as the most unstable structure there is; we should probably abandon it very shortly. We have all sorts of skyscrapers ready to go up without columns. I have a feeling that we only have to look at everything that is there, and not only at what we know.

May I remind you of an editorial by Mr. Peter Blake, who you know is an ex-editor of an ex-magazine, on architectural education? Apparently you cannot have several serious architectural magazines with criticism in America, you simply confuse things. Why would an advertiser of a simple commodity for sale or a simple business architect who is looking for how to do it buy such a magazine? Architectural magazines which are admirable catalogues, second only to Sweet's catalogue, have little to do with architectural criticism, history or theory. So by definition a profession which cannot sustain a magazine except for business purposes doesn't deserve a good magazine.

Forgive this aside. Back to the *Forum* and education. In an editorial about the many schools which were searching for new deans, Blake discussed various means of going about it. He mentioned among other things the star system resulting in part-time deanship instead of a whole-time administrative job. I would like to quote the last two paragraphs of his editorial and parts of my comments:

"The trouble is of course that education suffers as a result of all this and suffers very badly; for education has nothing to do with star-systems or competition for endowments. Education is a very serious business. It requires teachers dedicated and skilled at teaching and programs designed to turn students into professionals capable of dealing with tomorrow's problems, which will differ very radically from those faced by artist-architects skilled at producing exquisite but isolated monuments. It would be better for all concerned, for students, for faculty, for the country as a whole, if heads of architectural schools were picked not for their glamour but for their teaching ability, not in terms of one great man's style but in terms of the widest problems, social, economic, technological, as well as esthetic, that are likely to confront the profession in decades to come."

I commented in part: "The good and almost invariably needy student can now shop between several of the 'very best' schools for financial assistance. The fellowship and scholarship endowed school wins more often than not." This student really has to overcome something which is tacked on almost accidentally to his education. So the needy have to shop around for money, not for teaching. "Endowment is seldom if ever directly obtained in an architectural school. It is usually obtained by the university which does this for very general purposes, and I find in my experience, which is not inconsiderable, that the kitty is nearly always reserved for the more fashionable sciences and architecture gets short-changed, for the very simple reason that it is really still thought of as useless art." It actually isn't; it is a science as well as an art. And this again is a problem.

Architectural schools are still relatively poor and science schools relatively rich because the usefulness of the latter is immediately recognized, whereas architecture, even to very enlightened presidents, has a lower priority. The less enlightened, like most patrons, are satisfied to build with the help of the merely competent or decorators or status architects.

"Under any conditions of course, schools need good faculty as well as good students, and current practice in faculty appointment reflects the practices of the affluent society which is busy in the market place. The architects who teach practice first and teach second. (Historians are somewhat different; for they are on a full-time basis)." The voice of the market place has invaded the university sanctum. Many schools have become victims of the originally rational principle of practicing preachers, which has now become abused. In too many schools teaching salary has become subsidy for those waiting to get sufficient earning power to practice.

I don't of course intend this to be a general condemnation, there are exceptions to every rule; there are many teachers whose ideals and skills and integrity are beyond any question and who really are teachers first and foremost in spite of being successful practitioners. I have nothing against the master studio. I think one of the great advantages of the Beaux Art was this: students simply lived with the great man, and worked with him for three or four years, and even if he taught you nothing, even if he only grunted at you, almost by osmosis something was transfused of his genius through common involvement. The student knew everything about the man; he didn't have to justify himself in every encounter, you only were with him because you knew what he stood for and what he did; he didn't have to explain himself.

I am afraid I do not agree entirely with Mr. Zevi who suggested that a measured drawing is a voyage of discovery. Maybe he didn't intend this. The making of such a drawing is simply a way of inviting a very close examination of particulars, which is of course very important. But I think there is something more important even than that and living with a master. Anybody living in Rome or in any ancient, beautiful, historical environment absorbs a great deal and develops visual sensibility and judgment which may not be acquired at second hand. If you really live among lovely textures, shapes, colors and clear definitions between the man-made and nature you begin to understand the wholeness of man's habitat. The ugliness of our environment in the new industrial society is the biggest handicap under which the architects of the new world are suffering at this moment.

To add to what I said in that letter, we don't need more architectural schools as much as we need a great subsidy to the sensitive and talented—increasing direct subsidy through fellowships, loans or whatever other aids, together with absolutely free passportless exchanges and travel in a growing global society. We have to give people the opportunity to remain students, to stay out of the market place, and the privilege of being what they are, perhaps superior and sensitive hermits of our new world. We have to subsidize their advanced study and research in our field.

What we are doing at the present moment is reducing every student group to the lowest common denominator. This way we may not produce an appropriate education for architects of our time; neither do I think we shall produce practitioners fit for our time. Gropius became a great teacher because he had a purpose. He didn't have a special methodology or whatever; he had purpose, just simply that. He was a great teacher at the moment when teachers with fresh attitudes toward architectural responsibilities and potentials were needed. The Bauhaus was unquestionably very influential, and the students of the Bauhaus and the later Harvard and Institute of Design period, and many students of those periods who were not directly Bauhaus, Harvard or ID students benefitted enormously from this new turn in education.

Maybe we are in a comparable period when much questioning already is being done, by students more frequently than the faculty, as to whether current practices are really valid and if we have to re-evaluate the scope and nature of architecture in order to illuminate educational purpose. We cannot keep on tinkering with an architectural education in terms of courses when we don't see the end product that we are trying to get and nobody is ready to define it. It is quite evident to me that the broadened architecture, which is a loaded word, could with advantage be called by another name for the time being.

The entire spectrum of environmental design has been so widened, so immensely widened, that it is already out of the scope of any package deal in education. It is just too, too much.

It cannot be squeezed into four years and it cannot be squeezed into five years in which the last year is a "master" class so-called, but is really nothing but another unnecessary exercise for impatient boys, or a demonstration of premature genius, or just a finishing school for the status-seekers. This certainly is not education.

The first requirement is to use new tools for making educated men. This includes of course, education at the different levels of human development, which means that you have to re-formulate education, which we now think of as elementary education, or higher education or post-graduate education, into its proper doses in accordance with the individual human potential. Mind and character are formed in the pre-school years. If they are twisted then little can be done later to correct the deformation. It has been demonstrated that you can teach higher mathematics and languages very easily and simultaneously between the ages of eight and twelve. So then why should we wait until a child's capacity for learning certain things has been damaged and then try and stuff him like a goose for rich liver?

The real education we are talking about, of structuring or order-making, the comprehension of inter-relationship of things, must be pushed down as well as up. It implies an extension of the whole educational spectrum which is our concern in two directions, down below kindergarten and up into post-graduate research which may become a career in itself, as it is in every other field.

This notion pre-supposes a reparceling of learning-time. There is somewhere in the middle of this enlarged slice of learning and experience-gathering, and practice for certain people with demonstrable design ability, perhaps after two years of college, basic training, in making visible physical order or form. Two years of this would be good for future painters, graphic designers, photographers, sculptors, architects, urban designers and industrial designers, *et al.* We could go right back to the Bauhaus; we haven't invented anything better since. At the end of that period you would have found out who really stands out in creative or intellectual capacity, or in technical, analytical, logical capacity sufficiently to go on further towards more serious tasks in a chosen field. The purely facile, the gifted and talented could peel off and could become whatever "beautiful" image makers we need in society. Others would go into a technical two years in which exploration would be made of the ability to transform talent into systematic, purposeful action. They would receive an honorable degree as very useful functionaries in our society because we need a great many of them to translate imaginative thinking into actualities.

The remaining students could be asked to start originating —that is to say, to organize new complexity into new visible order. There might be two or three years in this course, including a year or two years of apprenticeship to be chosen by the student, not limited to going to the assemblage building construction industry, mixing skilled and advanced administrative ability and simple technology, but perhaps including the option to put together administrative ability and very advanced technology in production industry itself.

Finally, without any time limit at all, any properly qualified person could come back to research and study in environmental design and control in order to make the fullest use of the human resources and facilities of a great university. We would then have a diversity of *real* architects, who would be able to fill out the architectural spectrum. Some of these would be most particularly engaged in *special* interests and at the same time others would become *the most needed specialists of all, the men without particular involvement,* like the ideal President of the United States, men capable of making great decisions after being briefed by specialists, without being seduced by them.

THE CANON OF ARCHITECTURAL HISTORY

Sibyl Moholy-Nagy

No exciting exchange of opinions has ever resulted from a comparative evaluation of Hitler and Ghandi. Absolute evil and absolute good are dead issues. By the same token architectural eclecticism was absolute evil, and contemporaneousness absolute good in the architectural curriculum of a generation ago. The teaching of history was a dead issue and any debate about the relative merits of the departed would have made no sense.

It is an extraordinary phenomenon, not yet fully appreciated, that this corpse of architectural history has suddenly become the object of intense controversy, although contemporary convictions about teaching the absolute evil of eclecticism and the absolute good of contemporaneousness have not changed—Philip Johnson excepted. There are no heated debates about the pros and cons of bringing back the horse-drawn carriage or gas lighting because both have been superseded by effective innovations, school administrations, articles, and this very symposium is searching for answers to such questions as: Is there a workable history for practicing architects? Is the teaching of architectural history wasteful or essential? If we reinstate it as an important part of the undergraduate curriculum, is the traditional stylistic sequence—as represented by Bannister Fletcher and all other texts—a suitable tool?

The persistence and intensity of these inquiries permit only one conclusion—that the elimination or paralysis of history in architectural schools a generation ago has left a gap that, unlike horse-drawn carriages and gaslight, has not been replaced by a workable method, explaining to the student his place in the continuous phenomenon of man-made environment.

The question confronting us here and in our schools is therefore not whether architectural history is dead; it is obviously not. The question is what caused its eclipse, and what attitude or re-evaluation might help to prevent its imminent return from becoming a regressive disaster.

Francis Bacon called the study of history "a computation backward from our own time." At the very dawn of history as a science, he denied the objective interpretation, implying subjective, timebound selections from the past as a means to establish historical continuity. The desire—one might say, the *obsession*—to visualize this continuity in buildings is so universal among men that it amounts to a generic trait. Buried within Imhotep's seminal pyramid is a ziggurat. The social order of the Maya rested exclusively on time sequences, recorded in building projects. The Greeks emerged culturally only after deriving from Egyptian stone temples the visual basis for modulation and taming their volatile gods into pharaonic permanence. Rome taught Byzantium structure and plan articulation, and Byzantium taught Islam centralization and architectural symbolism. Islam taught the Gothic point support and lateral transference, and the Gothic taught iron construction, the fateful step from mass to point support and from weight to equilibrium. The Renaissance quarried its total vocabulary from three thousand years of tradition and transformation, and the Baroque exploded its logic by dematerializing it into a gigantic visual illusion. Like the runners of Marathon, culture handed on to culture the conceptual flame and the physical knowledge for the next link in the supra-real self-image that is architecture. Of all creatures only *homo sapiens* retains and reveres in the completed morphon of his ancestors the building blocks of an ever-changing man-made environment.

Although this causal chain of conceptual evolution is continuous from pre-history to our own time, its relationship to the training and the professional practice of architects underwent drastic changes some 150 years ago. Toward the close of the eighteenth century art history became an academic profession based on the classification of form phenomena grouped together as *styles*. Historical knowledge of buildings became iconographic. According to its semantic root iconography means the description and documentation of images. Extending this approach to historical buildings, the academic historian described and documented them on the basis of stylistic verisimilitude. It was a development that changed profoundly and permanently the meaning of architectural history for architects. Jefferson could still believe in an ulterior purpose of his measured drawings sent home from his studies of the Pantheon and the Maison Carrée. To him they were ideal public building types suitable for the new republic. And Pugin had no doubt that Gothic, faithfully rendered, would rekindle medieval piety. This expedient approach of the architect-historian was doomed when the appliqué style feature and the iconographically correct frontispiece became the ulterior purpose of teaching architectural history. It vitiated any assumption, still held astonishingly enough by some of our colleagues here, that architectural style is the legible imprint of socio-economic forces. Architectural form and any architectural theory behind it are so relative in their interpretation as to be unrelated to any ascertainable reality. It is well to remember that admiration for Classicism produced identical triplets in Stalin's Moscow, Hitler's Germany, and Roosevelt's Washington.

The effect of this splitting-off of analytical historical knowledge from constructive architectural purpose can be explained with an analogy from economics. In the early stages of capitalism, called primitive accumulation, the owner of wealth saw the incentive for its accumulation in the possibility of spending it on personal wish-fulfillment, benefitting in the process the wealth of the community. In the mature phase of capitalism wealth is accumulated for the sole purpose of producing more wealth, which is channelled back into an abstract system of investments and corporate profits, totally divorced from any personal wish-fulfillment or immediate benefit to the community. In the same way, architects of the pre-academic phase accumulated historical capital to spend it for the benefit of fulfilling their design vision, benefitting in the process the collectively held architectural ideals of the community. In the academic phase, the sole incentive for the accumulation of art-historical capital is the accumulation of more art-historical capital, a self-perpetuating processing of iconographic data and documents for the sake of more iconographic data and documents. Sworn into tenure on established style theorems, the iconographic historian must select and interpret particulars by a process of deduction from *a priori* stylistic truths.

As new building needs stimulated new materials and methods, an ever increasing number of architects left the art-historical morgue in digust. They initiated a new design phase which, for the first time in Western history, drew exclusively from contemporary resources. Forty years after this open split between the practicing architect and the incestuous architectural historian, it is possible to evaluate the results of this revolution against the misuses of the past. The sum total, which is what counts more in the composite image of an epoch than the unique masterpiece of the genius, amounts to a preponderance of repetitive box shapes of impermanent materials and construction. Their design never rose above a subtractive purism, incapable of replacing the eliminated historical appeal with a new aesthetics. This so-called new architecture has created a featureless environment of hand-crafted machine products, belonging neither to architecture as art nor to architecture as technology, neither to history nor to the future.

The failure of the International Style to stimulate either the creative imagination of the architect, *or* provide identification for the client, *or* answer to the need for historical consciousness in cityscapes, was the immediate cause for the reanimation of the historical corpse. It was a revival that did not start in the most logical place—the schools of architecture, which, at least in America, are servile camp followers of every trend and not makers of architectural revolutions. The rediscovery of architectural continuity must be credited to practicing architects and the most successful ones at that. Saarinen was perhaps the first one with his Lombardizing chapel at MIT, followed by Johnson, Rudolph, Kahn, Weese, Johansen, Yamasaki—even by Gropius, the celebrated Medicine Man of international Functionalism. They all tried kaleidoscopic combinations of historical and contemporary elements in an attempt to recover architecture from between the teeth of building technology. The results have been rarely successful, and frequently ridiculous. We are beyond recall of past forms, no matter how tastefully updated. The artless ingenuity with which earlier times enriched themselves on the perfect solution is lost forever because architects today are the product of the anti-stylistic revolt, whether they participated in it or not. Whatever readaptation they try is done with a bad conscience. It is old sin poorly rationalized as new virtue.

It is here that architectural theory reveals its total futility for learning or practicing architects. Theory is generalized principle, analyzing reality. The whole vast body of generalized principle, from Vitruvius to Banham, refers *backward* to established architectural facts. It can never refer forward to future design solutions. The danger of the new historical wave is not, as Gropius naively assumed at the Bauhaus, the inhibition of budding architectural self-expression by past genius. He obviously knew nothing of the educational process based on the vital tension between the admired precedent and painful self-liberation. The danger is the theoretical justification of the stylistic crutch.

What then is the role, if any, of architectural history, without which the architect seems unable to survive as the creative leader in man's unending search for at-homeness on his earth? I propose that we have reached a crucial point in architectural development where we must face the conscious effort of shaping a new link in the chain of architectural continuity that binds the past to the future. This new link will receive its strength not from adaptation but from apprehension, not from a knowledge of past solutions but from a comprehension of historical concepts, fused into an amalgam in which historical and contemporary are synonymous.

Schools, responsible for the implementation of such a new link, must discard in their history courses "stylistic attributes" as arbitrary and extraneous.

The *typical* Greek portico, the *typical* Roman town plan, the *typical* Gothic vault, all existed in a hundred different combinations long before they were forced into an illegitimate union with socio-political time sequences. Architectural continuity has a historical time sequence of its own which is totally independent of chapter headings in history books. While the beaver, the tent caterpillar and the nautilus may be our equals in structural imagination, man as architect has the unique ability to invest a universal idea with a perceptive form. The result of this process is a *designed concept* that is analogous to itself and to nothing else. It is purely architectural because it responds in purely architectural terms to environment as being expedient, intellectual and emotional, as sensuous and spiritual, as pre-planned and spontaneous, as collective and individual, historical and contemporary, and most of all as organic beyond nature.

While style attributes are as numerous as the art historians who invent them, the basic concepts of architecture are few—

five, speaking historically, and six, if we consider our own epoch as already belonging to the continuity of time. The five past historical concepts are, in the order of their emergence:

> *Verticality*
> *Space Progression*
> *Modulation and Modification*
> *Structured Planning*
> *Art-space Symbolism*

For almost a thousand years the accumulated substance of these five concepts was rich enough to serve the architectural self-image of each epoch in innumerable configurations. Neither Islam nor Romanesque, neither Gothic, Renaissance nor Baroque added a new basic concept to the vocabulary of Western architecture, evolved over four thousand years. Almost another millenium would have to pass till the outlines of a sixth basic concept are starting to emerge. This sixth concept, now in its infancy and not yet assured of either historical significance or creative excellence, is *Space-form Continuity*—the changed course of architectural continuity from the third to the fourth dimension.

The cumulative effect of the five primary concepts on the history of architecture may be likened, somewhat loosely, to a musical canon. Each subsequent voice takes up the harmony of the previous one with a different interval; but in contrast to the musical term, each addition to the architectural canon is completely original. Other analogies are possible: the complex organism of a beehive, for instance, whose survival and well-functioning depend on a harmonizing of decidely different life factors. Architecturally speaking it all adds up to a cumulative force of conceptual selections of which none is ever obsolete because all are predicated on the human condition. As long as man is body, dependent on gravity, oxygen, protection, food intake, perambulation, and group contact, he will look to architecture for an ideal environment that will minimize this physical bondage for the release of non-physical potentialities. This is the eternal presence of architecture.

Someone once said that a program says what next and why; it does not specify the how, who, or when. I would take up an inordinate amount of your time if I broke this rule and established now concept by concept historical sequences from inception through growth and maturity to the point where a new concept encroaches, and a merger occurs that still influences the architecture we design today. I had intended to show you some slides, most of them familiar to you, that would merely establish the visual identity of verticality, space progression, modulation and modification, structured planning, art-space symbolism, and space-form continuity. Since our location and timing are un-suited for projection, I shall attempt a verbal snapshot of three concepts, hoping that a book in progress will bear out the im-portance I attach to these basic concepts in the process of archi-tectural education.

Verticality

Verticality first appears in Mesopotamia, in Sumer, to be precise. It is fully developed when archeology limps into the picture, uncounted generations behind the beginning of urban civilization and its *leitmotif* of verticality. It derives from man's desire to free himself from dependence on the earth crust and the chthonian forces below it. By its chronological primogeni-ture, verticality amounts to a *first cause* of architecture.

The first fully developed ziggurat establishes the difference between height and verticality. With the equilateral pyramid of Egypt, verticality becomes abstract. The counter-point is es-tablished: accessible and symbolic verticality—Greek pediment and Islamic minaret—Lombard campanile and Gothic *fléche*. The alternatives at the disposal of architecture today: the height of a Pan Am building or a World Trade Center against the verticality of a Seagram Building or Sert's student housing on the Charles River. Verticality as accessible experience: the Gug-genheim Museum ramp; and verticality as pure symbol: Saari-nen's gateway arch in St. Louis.

Space progression

The origin of space progression is found in Egypt, in Imho-tep's colonnade at Sakkarah. The Sumerian star-bound city-state has made way for a hierarchic order, taking possession of the earth in the name of divine order. The measured procession through the first enclosures is not organic nature but man-made spaces. They are proportionless then because man passes through; he does not dwell yet. Gradually—it takes more than a thousand years—space progression becomes related to man instead of God, it becomes bi-axial, multicellular, and the second architectural concept is born: *enfilade*. Crete, the Iranian Bit Hilani, the multiple agoras of the Hellenistic city, beget the Roman fora and the enfilade of the Roman villa. A long eclipse. Medieval man has been told by the church that he does not dwell here any more. The Renaissance aligns space progression along the magic perspective line but only Baroque recovers the reciprocal vista, the sophisticated light articulation of Karnak.

Analogous to our mix-up of height and verticality, space progression has been reduced to space addition in our own time: Miesian corridor lofts, or the vistaless stemmed cubicles of Kahn's "spaces within spaces." But the architectural memory of the race never forgets completely. Niemeyer's Palace of the Dawn in Brasilia is pure enfilade, Johnson's Utica Museum makes a tentative attempt, as does Rudolph's villa in Jacksonville. Burle Marx has recovered it in two gardens in Petropolis, but only the Plaza Cubierta of the University of Caracas comes close to the initial concept of space progression, the light articulated enfilade of Deir el-Bahri.

Modulation and modification

I shall merely mention modulation and modification, added by the Greeks to the canon of architectural history by inventing the anthropometric scale. They alone measured form in search of ideal equations, modifying architecture as cosmic image. Rome received the man-centered message but broke through the modulated form of Greece into *planned spaces, interdependent with structure*. In a way Zevi was right when years ago he asserted that it is with the structured spaces of Rome that architecture starts.

The fifth of the historical concepts lifts verticality, enfilade, modulation and structured planning off their foundations and carries them into a celestial vacuum created by the Byzantine church.

Art-space symbolism

It is here more than with the preceding concepts that a mere mention must be enough, in the absence of visualization. The tension between the hidden meaning and the logos is resolved through applied geometry, and the blatant truth of geometry is veiled by *kosmesis*—the blending of symbolic structure and symbolic art. Le Corbusier's Ronchamp comes close to the same sequence of the hermetic truth and the evident path toward it— the integral adornment symbolic of a structural logos. But this must be written in illustrations. There are no words for art as symbolic catalyst.

In conclusion I shall barely touch on the sixth concept I see as a potential contribution of our own time to the historical continuity of architecture.

Space-form continuity

This is not a non-historical concept. Past epochs got intimations of its possibilities—the interacting space definitions of Hadrian's Villa, or the primitive phase of the space age—the early eighteenth century, expressing a dawning cosmic consciousness in kinetic-dynamic sensations—staircases spiralling into voids, the participation of the imaginative eye in the dispersion of architectural enclosure. But the earthbound rationality of the five tangible concepts always succeeded in a renewed three-dimensional persuasion. Architecture remains orbicular around the static human center. Inner and outer space are separately defined.

To a new generation these definitions seem insufficient, and Geoffrey Scott's "delight of three dimensions" no longer the *only* environmental delight. The configuration of space seems suddenly thrown upon ourselves, our movement, the participation of our perceptive senses in the passage of time through space. And this space no longer strikes against solids. In a perceptive reversal solids form the edges of spaces, cut tangentially by movement. These are intimations of a new conceptual link —the visualization of time through architecture. Le Corbusier's ramp thrown across the undefined space of the Carpenter Center for the Visual Arts, Harvard University, seems a sort of beacon pointing toward realization. Saarinen's TWA Terminal indicates the future, and the astounding section through Scharoun's Berlin Symphony Hall. Frei Otto's tent structures and Soleri's Mesa City are perhaps closest to space-form continuity as the new link in the history of architecture.

None of the five historical concepts is invalidated by this possible conquest of a fourth dimension. The architectural canon is that much richer and surer of its impact through a new harmony.

I think of Bergson's sunburst, scattering particles of sidereal substance over the universe to form new stars in different amalgams of the mother substance, each nucleus a concept that is the eternal presence. This is what architectural history offers me as a teacher of future architects—conceptual evidence of change in permanence. I can see no other meaning in it.

HISTORY: AN ORIENTATION
FOR THE ARCHITECT

Stephen W. Jacobs

*History is necessary not only to make life agreeable, but also to
endow it with moral significance. (Marsilio Ficino)*

In this paper I propose to offer answers to some of the
questions suggested for discussion by the organizers of this
seminar in their letter of invitation to the speakers. First of all,
is history of architecture different for the architect from what
it is for the general public? In other words, is the interest
in architectural history of the producer unlike that of the consumer? Dr. Banham reminds us that many believe history "has
hung on" in schools of architecture "as a way of 'getting a bit
of culture into the course'." This view implies that it is no more
significant for the architecture student than for any other par-
ticipant in our culture.[1]

On the other hand, we are often told that really great works
are "universal"—presumably as accessible and valuable to the
layman as the architect. Thus it is often argued on the basis of
these common notions from opposite ends of the producer-
consumer spectrum, that history of architecture is not significantly different for the practitioner than for the layman. If we
accept this conclusion, as many of our leading institutions do
(either as a matter of happenstance or of policy), a number of
consequences important for history and for school curricula
ensue. It becomes logical to divorce the discussion of architectural tradition from the professional school context and to
place it among the liberal arts. It seems natural to employ
trained historians as teachers—men who have learned art historical method without special reference to the technical, structural, social, and organizational problems which affect architecture alone among the visual arts. Architectural history may
then become a dreary appendage of the history of painting
program, or, sometimes more disastrous, the province of provo-

---

[1] Reyner Banham, "Historical Studies and Architectural Criticism," *Outlet* (Bart-
lett School Magazine), No. 55 (1964), p. 46.

cative performers with literary flair and dramatic style. It is the thesis of this paper that a proper concern for architectural history requires that the professional schools maintain a close liaison with its ongoing process.

If architectural students are to be given a proper orientation —a sense of where they come upon the scene, and what the accumulated experience of the profession is and may mean— they must learn about existing architectural products in a way which recognizes and capitalizes on their special interests, potentials, and concerns. Not only must the teachers and graduates of architecture schools attempt to "make" architectural history but they must understand it. They must understand its virtues and limitations as an art form dependent on the marshalling of facts and observations. They must be aware of its hybrid character, combining with their own major medium of communication, the universal visual language, the verbal symbolic language of a local culture. They must see architectural history not as presenting a succession of selected "examples" in an imaginary museum but as one of the significant means of gaining insight. History must give them the understanding they need to approach particular communities or architectural situations where they may find themselves among the tourists, decision-makers or form givers. It must also provide the basis for a personal formulation, a sense of the relevance of large scale objects both to natural and artificial conditions and to human activities and potentials. It should give them a basis of comparison for the establishment of standards, for the judgment of quality, appropriateness, and long range viability in their own works and those of others. As Giedion puts it, "History is not a compilation of facts, but an insight into a moving process of life."[2]

The problem is compounded by the "special" nature of the architect, and the tendency of enterprising architectural students of our day to regard themselves as artists rather than building technicians, social reformers, systems specialists, or businessmen. The profession, the trade journals, and the public myth all encourage our budding architects to develop their "talent" rather than to submerge in the "life-adjustment" expected of others.

---

[2] S. Giedion, *Space, Time and Architecture*. (Cambridge, Mass., 1941), p. v.

Our "problem solvers" are admired not so much for their effiiciency or the economy of their means (as, for instance, is true of engineers) as for the striking nature of their product and the lasting value of their formulation. It is memorability which is the goal today, an "image" based on perception and experience of the solution, modified by verbalizations about it and assumptions and inhibitions brought to the transaction by the various observers. Whether the structure survives is relatively unimportant. In her extraordinary essay on "The Crisis in Culture", Hannah Arendt observes that "the last individual left in a mass society seems to be the artist."[3]

All others are "mass men" who no longer can escape to a variety of "out" groups, the established revolutionary nuclei to which idealists have repaired in the past. "A good part of the despair of individuals under the conditions of mass society is due to the fact that these avenues of escape are now closed because society has incorporated all strata of the population."[4]

The peculiar consequences of this dichotomy between the artist and his society include not only the well-known phenomenon of philistinism, familiar since the development of utilitarian "middle-class values" in the eighteenth century. Consumption of art, and, recently, vicarious participation in it, have become a recognized means of escape. Miss Arendt makes a further distinction important for our understanding of the situation of the architect of our day and the role which history education must play in preparing him to make the most of it. She maintains that the traditional hierarchical society may have "abused" cultural objects, devaluing them to "social commodities," but that it did not destroy them completely. Their husks remain to be resurrected by historians and other "wasteland" wanderers. "Mass society, on the contrary, wants not culture but entertainment, and the wares offered by the entertainment industry are indeed consumed by society just like any other consumer goods. . . . . The commodities the entertainment industry offers are not 'things,' cultural objects, whose excellence is measured by their ability to withstand the life process and

---

[3] Hannah Arendt, *Between Past and Future: Six Exercises in Political Thought.* (New York, 1961), p. 200.

---

[4] *Ibid.* p. 141.

become permanent appurtenances of the world, and they should not be judged according to these standards; nor are they values which exist to be used and exchanged; they are consumer goods, destined to be used up, just like any other consumer goods."[5]

Thus our architects are presented with a dilemma more difficult to resolve than that of any other contemporary artists. Because "mass culture" is oriented towards entertainment and/or education, it rewards the distributor, not the creator. Planned obsolescence as well as normal commercial exploitation of the meretricious are the order of the day in mass culture. Under these circumstances success, which vulgarizes the creative work in a manner undreamed of by the naive popularizers of the past, is more fatal than oblivion. To capitalize on the conditions of the moment, the serious artist must be more mobile and individualistic than ever in the past, and he must expect to see his original contribution widely disseminated before it has had time to mature or develop its potential. In view of the widespread interest in the activities of this renegade subculture, even the operatic anonymity of the "misunderstood" nineteenth-century garret painter is denied the contemporary artist. Because of the social nature of his work, and the need to persuade others to invest in it, the architect who has no aversion to publicity has more to gain from public interest than the others. For the same reasons, his work cannot be as ephemeral or irresponsible as the product of other manipulators of the visible. He is forced to be conscious not only of the need for a momentary, cathartic "self-expression" to be flung to the pursuing culture consumers like the golden apples of Atalanta, but also to provide for the more specialized and concrete needs of clients and captive audiences who cannot avoid his product or replace it as regularly as the works of other visual or literary artists. Until now the architecture of the absurd has generally been inadvertent.

Given the nature of the problem—the teaching of architectural history to architects in such a manner that they become aware of their role as creative producers whose products endure longer and may have more kinds of impact than any other consumer items of our day—we may still wonder whether such teaching should, in fact, be different from that provided for

---

[5] *Ibid*, pp. 205-206.

the culture-conscious mass. My conclusion is that it should include all the perceptual training, categorical constructs, interpretative information, formal analysis, and consideration of trends, personalities, iconography, psychoses, and media which normally form a part of such a program, plus more besides. The program to which the architect is subjected should never completely forget the awful fact that this very person is to commit architecture.

History for the architect must go beyond the normal history of architecture program in four ways: it must be more concerned with the sources and rationales of existing solutions; it must consider the full gamut of materials, techniques, and schemes now tested by use; it must pay greater attention to the attitudes and messages of consumers and producers in the past; it must be concerned with the how and why as well as the usual what, where, when, and who. In other words, appreciation is not enough. To be valuable to the architect, to provide adequate orientation for him, history must give him a sense of involvement. It must show him the frontiers of his field and give him the means of understanding his role. It must make clear the relation of his life and activities to those of others, both living and dead. These concerns may, in fact, be conveyed to some degree by the usual scholarly history course. But unless it is consciously planned for, this is not likely to be the case.

Still other responsibilities in the education of architects have fallen by default to history. They are peripheral to history, but nonetheless important. At present most curricula do not provide a viable philosophical base for their students' activities or hopes as the future shapers of the environment. Even though "Theory" is traditionally listed and presented, most informed observers maintain that there is no valid statement of principle generally agreed to and available to the architect as a usable set of assumptions. Sir John Summerson points out that architectural theory has its own dialectic divorced from the production of architecture and must be taught chronologically as a history of architectural ideas.[6]

Unless the teaching staff includes an erudite fellow who can

---

[6] John Summerson, "The Case for a Theory of Modern Architecture," *Journal of the Royal Institute of British Architects,* 3rd series, LXIV (June 1957), pp. 307-310.

make clear the historic arguments of architecture, awareness for the architect of the identifiable issues even in his own limited field must be gleaned from the history program. Similarly, unless he is required to take a broad-gauge philosophy course (neither semanticizing nor positivist), the architect's only understanding of traditional human intellectual concerns may be an unplanned byproduct of history course work.

Another burden which history has often been forced to assume (in the undergraduate curricula for architects at least) is the development of verbal skills and maintenance of minimal literacy. Few other parts of the professional training program for architects require intelligent reading (as against handbook learning or the old Bannister Fletcher tradition). Carefully prepared written reports are rarely required. Because of its concern for integrating verbal and visual communications, the history program demonstrates strikingly the deterioration of the students' verbal skills in the course of the normal architectural curriculum, where energies and interest are concentrated on the design program, generally to the detriment of academic performance in regular course work. Since architectural practice does require considerable sales ability—verbal as well as visual—architectural education cannot afford to ignore the role of propaganda, of written and oral communication, in preparing students for a field in which "the message" is a major artistic concern. As Steen Eiler Rasmussen points out, the architect as organizer of the building may not be able to communicate on all levels since "architecture is incapable of communicating an intimate personal message from one person to another." Rather, he is forced to clarify and simplify his ideas to make them effective when embodied in buildings.[7] Developing semantic procedures to parallel the drafting-board formulation is important both in working with colleagues and clients and in publicizing the solution. And beyond this it is generally recognized that "architects must be liberally educated and broadly informed."[8]

Recognition of the problems of providing adequate philo-

---

[7] Steen Eiler Rasmussen, *Experiencing Architecture.* (Cambridge, Mass., 1964), p. 14. Some of our more "original" architects have yet to get the message.
[8] Albert Bush-Brown, "About Books not yet Written," *Journal of the American Institute of Architects,* XXXIV (November 1960), p. 59.

sophic and literary experience to neophyte architects has reinforced the trend towards graduate professional education. This is in line with the patterns now established in most other professional disciplines. Yet there is reason to believe that for designers, as for mathematicians, we defer involvement at considerable peril. Once launched, architects tend to develop their skills and to make their contribution over a long period of time. In fact it is possible to demonstrate that for an architect to become "great" he must live to a ripe age. In this architects are unlike mathematicians. However, like the latter, architects who are diverted from their primary concerns during their college years may find their budding skills, their ability to make significant new formulations, withering on the vine. There is reason to suspect that architects who undertake their training at the graduate level fail to develop the design fluency which they could have attained by continued involvement during their formative years (perhaps not to the exclusion of everything else) in design. In any event, whether for graduate or undergraduate architects, history today should encourage verbal expression and intelligent discussion. This should be a major consideration and part of the planned student response to the material. This is essential where other parts of the student's program are primarily professional. It is, of course, tempting to have spatial diagrams, models, or sketches prepared by the students. Often architects are better able to express themselves in this manner. The results are quickly evaluated, and may serve as useful teaching tools. However, this kind of submission is more valuable for the nonprofessional student who lacks experience in architectonic visualization than for the student who is presumably devoting much of his time and attention to such matters. The architecture student must be encouraged to read and write, not only for his own salvation, but for that of the profession.

The argument, then, is that history *is* different for the architect. It is not one of a great many useful educational tools he may choose to pick up, but a vital source of knowledge about the achievements and background of the profession and of the world in which it operates. It will not enable him to emulate the styles or attitudes of others, but rather is a source of insight which helps him to understand the nature of his opportunities and his role. If the course is developed with architects in mind, it may also provide useful experience in verbalizing about architecture, in the consideration of significant issues in the field, and an awareness of the assumptions, values, and social aspirations which underlay the decisions and dreams of architects. It will assume and encourage a serious interest in structures, materials, and mechanical developments. It will stress social aspects —pathology as well as civic pride, planning as well as landscape, programs and procedures as well as forms. It will attempt to help the architect to become a responsible as well as a creative organizer of the environment.

What place should the history of painting and sculpture have in the curriculum?

We owe to French social historians of the early nineteenth century our sense of the interaction of a great variety of kinds of historical evidence. As Michelet put it to Sainte-Beuve in 1837, "If I had introduced only political history into my narrative, if I had taken no account of the diverse elements of history (religion, law, geography, literature, art, etc.), my procedure would have been quite different. But a great vital movement was needed, because all these elements gravitated together in the unity of the story."[9]

History of architecture courses too must profit from "the diverse elements of history," and, to the extent that they are significant to the development of architecture and unfamiliar to the students, a wide variety of related materials from other historical areas must be introduced. To be effective, the presentation of architecture should include selected painting and sculpture. This is especially true of those monuments (such as Gothic cathedrals or Greek temples) much of whose character derives from the carved ornament or the painted glass, and of works (like those of the early 20th century) which owe their vocabulary of forms to the experimental art of their day. In some instances (Michelangelo, Bernini, Le Corbusier), the creative personality of the architect cannot be adequately considered without references to his works in painting and sculpture. "The physical reality of the spatial arts makes for complexity; nature is prolific with its materials, and one artist may work with media

---

[9] Marc Bloch, *The Historian's Craft.* (New York, 1953), p. 154.

so diverse in character that it becomes difficult to detect common traits of personality. . . ."[10] Thus a certain amount of overlap between architectural and art history must be anticipated. In the introductory courses it should be sought for.

It is particularly important to include painting and sculpture material in the early phases of the history program so that students will become aware of the interrelation of the various arts. In some cases (possibly the discussion of the Rococo or the Mycenaean) it is well to include the minor arts so that an awareness of the gamut of traditional artifacts is developed. But this will not be accomplished in the normal compartmentalized system, where architectural historians stick to their last and it is necessary to enroll in a specialized course (usually in another department) in order to find out about the parallel developments in painting. The answer is a carefully organized introductory course, one tailored to reflect the special interests and talents of available personnel and the situation of the students.

Once the architectural student has been made aware of the interaction of the arts and has a frame of reference in terms of time, place, societies and heroes, it would be well to give him some options in his historical studies. He should not be expected to "cover" all aspects of all the arts in detail but should be encouraged to enroll in specialized or general courses in the history of painting and sculpture to the extent that he has time and inclination to do so. Other things being equal, the architecture student tends today to gravitate towards modern painting, oriental art, and general surveys of sculpture as his preferred subject matter. The presence of distinctive personalities, outstanding courses, or local resources may attract interest to a wide range of other relatively specialized offerings. For the intelligent student, exposure to differing attitudes, procedures and problems in consideration of a variety of artistic subcultures is more important than authoritative knowledge about a limited segment of the artistic tradition or a monotonously systematic consideration of the whole. There are three major objectives. The first is to gain an understanding of the potential of specific works of art and the scholarly study of them. Second is expe-

---

[10] James S. Ackerman, "Western Art History," in James S. Ackerman and Rhys Carpenter, *Art and Archaeology.* (Englewood Cliffs, N. J., 1963), p. 137.

rience in using the library materials relating to works of art and architecture. Third is the assessment of the effect and significance of historic works of art both for their own day and ours.

Since all of these activities relate to and reinforce the history of architecture program, the specialized history of art courses can be interspersed almost at random with the intermediate or advanced history of architecture courses. The one rule that must be kept in mind is that no student should be encouraged to embark on two history courses at the same time. It does not matter whether one or both are history of architecture rather than history of art. Architecture students never do as well in two history courses taken concurrently as they would if they were taken separately. Even gifted students have difficulty keeping track of two sets of history materials while involved in other aspects of the professional curriculum. At least one of the history courses suffers.

Our conclusion, then, is that the history of painting and sculpture have an important role to play in the architecture curriculum. They must be shown to be relevant from the beginning of the student's indoctrination by inclusion of painting and sculpture material in the introductory history courses, thus giving a sense of the continuities characteristic of the various visual arts as well as of the distinctive qualities which make it possible to regard them as specialized fields. Once a firm frame of reference is established, students should be encouraged to take the initiative in discovering the course offerings in the history of art which speak to their condition.

Is the history of architecture the same discipline as the history of art?

History, as a discipline, has a considerable history and is still evolving. Based on the witnesses of the past accessible to us in the present, its goal is knowledge of human circumstance and activity.[11]

Since the development of photography the role of the arts as historic witness has grown rapidly until now it impinges on the traditional primacy of the written materials of history. The

---

[11] For a concise statement of the nature of history and the qualities required of the historian, see Charles Samaran, *L'Histoire et ses Methodes*. ("Encyclopedie de la Pleiade"), XI (Bruges, 1961), pp. XII-XIII.

modification of such magisterial efforts as the *Cambridge Histories,* which have included larger and larger masses of archaeological and photographic evidence with succeeding editions, indicates the trend. It is gradually being made clear to conventional historians what is rarely said by them—that artifacts are better historic evidence than writings. Despite the woeful lack of visual literacy among our scholars and the deplorable failure to require consideration of visual phenomena as part of the contemporary liberal education, more and more people are becoming aware of the "language of vision" as a universal medium of communication.[12]

Artifacts now visible may still appear as they did when they were made yesterday or in prehistoric times. Inevitably, many objects, whether works of art or architecture, show the ravages of time and decay. But the latter are generally impersonal forces, and their actions can be predicted and sometimes reversed if proper methods are available or reconstructions are made. The objects we see—particularly those discovered by archaeological means—have not been preselected for us by witnesses whose points of view and biases are inevitably different from our own. We are not faced with verbal reports in a variety of languages which may themselves have been modified over the years. We do not have to take someone else's word for it, as we inevitably must in acquiring political history. We can see for ourselves. Without benefit of Latin, Greek, Sanskrit or Tagalog, we have accessible to us the efforts of the great and minor masters in all the arts, either in the original, or, increasingly, in photographic form.

The establishing of the facts regarding historic works either of art or of architecture is now a well-known process. The subsequent synthesis and presentation of the findings, the second part of the historian's job, is similar for both. Obviously historians of art and architecture have much in common; frequently individuals are active in both fields (Anthony Blunt, Rudolf Wittkower, James Ackerman). Art and architectural

[12] Gyorgy Kepes, *Language of Vision.* (Chicago, 1944). While it is not necessary to accept the Gestalt view of aesthetics nor Kepes' conclusions about tasks faced by creative artists of his generation, this work remains an excellent guide to avant-garde visual communication of the first half of the twentieth century.

history must be regarded as separate specialties rather than distinct disciplines.

Is it desirable or necessary that a historian of architecture be an architect?

For all comers the historical process must be similar. On the one hand is the raw material—the buildings embodying concepts, displaying forms, exploiting structures, marshalling materials, covered with textures, containing volumes, relating spaces, providing for activities, affected by natural and artificial illumination, weathering and use—all combined with varying proportions, colors, mass, and rhythm. This is the stable part of the equation. On the other hand is the human observer—sometimes blind or obtuse, but possibly responsive to pleasure, protection, variety, surprise, balance, grandeur, motion, warmth, space, excitement or echo. The historian is the go-between, encouraging the observer to experience or imagine architectural forms and then to understand them. It is his function to organize the evidence, to select and present, to annotate and illuminate, to describe and discuss the individual instances which are the ultimate data. It is he who categorizes and orders, who helps others to see not only the aesthetic appeal of architecture, but its relevance to past and present and its role as witness. He should be willing and able to carry on, and perhaps teach, the normal art-historical procedures—including analysis of form, investigation of iconography, and connoisseurship.[13] But he must have other concerns, as well as knowledge which is most readily gained in the study or practice of architecture.

A. L. Rowse has indicated where the divergence of the two specialties occurs. He points out that "there are two ways of regarding" the history of all the arts and sciences. "There is the history of the art or science as a technical discipline in itself —whether architecture or music, medicine or chemistry—and there is its history viewed as a product of a given society, reflecting its demands, needs and circumstances. You may see this approach in any good history of architecture—perhaps the most social of the arts, the art in which the social element is at its highest. . . ."[14]

---

[13] James S. Ackerman, *op. cit.*, p. 160.
[14] A. L. Rowse, *The Use of History*. (London, 1963), p. 65.

Since the consideration of architecture as cultural evidence differs in degree rather than kind from the consideration of other art forms in this connection, it should be relatively easy for the non-architect art historian to develop an appreciation for the special involvement of architecture with its social context. Discussion of the "technical discipline" of architecture is obviously more difficult for the historian who has had no previous contact with architectural education or practice. Lack of technical and professional knowledge may be a serious handicap. There have been many occasions when learned and distinguished art historians have expatiated on "the expression of structure" in a manner which made all too clear their fundamental inability to distinguish between expression and structure. Inevitably, the art historian who has no special liaison with the profession will tend to be consumer rather than producer oriented, to emphasize the what at the expense of the how, and perhaps to misunderstand the why.

It is now taken for granted that the architectural historian must have special training beyond that provided by the normal architecture curriculum. Some go so far as to suppose that architectural experience may constitute a hazard, indicating a lamentable lack of scholarly dedication, a parochial view, and a discursive method. We have all been exposed to the well-intentioned traveler among the design critics who presents a history of Renaissance architecture as a travelog, using the splendid color slides he made on summer tours, and relying on Bannister Fletcher (plus, perhaps, a little Giedion and Pevsner) for his expertise. The resulting superficial review is still characteristic of many architecture programs in outlying schools. As one particularly bitter scholar put it, he objected to architectural history "being taught by frustrated architects." More attention should be paid to the problems of acquiring and holding qualified history of architecture staff in our professional schools.

Strangely enough, our historic tradition in history of architecture emphasizes the unusual accomplishment of the architect-scholar in the field. It is only in the history of architecture that American scholars have made art-history contributions which can rival those of the European originators of the discipline.[15]

---

[15] Ackerman, *op. cit.*, p. 192.

From Howard Crosby Butler through Kenneth Conant and Henry-Russell Hitchcock most of our distinguished performers have had professional training in architecture more extensive than their specific training for history. A sense of the material realities may have been an especially valuable acquisition in the pre-scientific days when "the history of art was taught as an adjunct to ethics or simply to the gentlemanly life . . . [and] offered no stimulus to either criticism or scholarship."[16]

But professional background without art historical scholarship is not enough. In an earlier day, when eclecticism in architecture was directed towards a wider range of historic precedents than is normal for our more masochistic age, it was possible to be sentimental rather than scholarly in "adapting" historic forms. "Historic atmosphere" was sought rather than consistency. The architect Joy Wheeler Dow, in his characteristic book on *The American Renaissance,* suggests that he was prepared to capitalize on "the salutary influence of whatever has been good in past buildings epochs."[17] He did not make entirely clear what constituted the "good" but assumed that his readers were sufficiently imbued with Victorian morality and acquisitiveness to find his remark acceptable and his tasteful potpourris of historic architectural forms suitable as turn-of-the-century suburban dwellings. Not for him the painstaking and noncommittal "empirical method" which has dominated the study and practice of the history of architecture since the great migration of European scholars in the 1930's.

It was as a reaction to the uninformed enthusiasms of the aesthetes that rigorous art-historical scholarship of the Warburg-Courtauld-Institute-of-Fine-Arts kind was established. Regarding art history as an adjunct of social science, and influenced by the determinist theories of history which were so influential in the politics as well as the arts of the era, these scholars applied the patterns of organization and used the investigative tools of linguists, archaeologists, psychologists, medical technicians, sociologists and crime-busters. They demonstrated that the art or architectural historian must be not only a form analyst and connoisseur (as the American tradition established in the Ivy

[16] Ackerman, *ibid.,* p. 141.
[17] Joy Wheeler Dow, *The American Renaissance.* (New York, 1904), preface, pp. 114, 127.

League universities insisted) but also a cultural historian and an iconographer.[18]

It is in the two latter areas that the architectural historian who has not had the benefit of indoctrination in historical method is likely to be weakest. And since they do not necessarily appear elsewhere in the architect's training (form awareness and the development of acuity and "taste" are important byproducts of most good studio courses in design) it is particularly important that the historian emphasize cultural context and the potentials of symbolic and other kinds of communication in architecture.

On the other hand, the teaching which art-historical scholars are now prepared to provide is unpalatable, and, possibly, unsuited for most architecture students. Furthermore, as Dr. Banham points out, these specialists tend to consider other approaches to historical indoctrination of architects necessarily inferior and probably anti-intellectual.[19]

The trained art historian as we now know him—the specialist scholar of the new dispensation—is a thoroughly academic type, oriented towards the procedures and the minutely specialized problems of his particular area. He expects systematic work and careful digestion of facts and forms from his students. This individual is unhappy in the professional school. He finds the extraordinary "boom or bust" pattern of architectural education intolerable. He cannot accept or adjust to the fact that his students perform and perhaps attend irregularly, attempting to catch up in the intervals between design crises. He finds the isolation from his group and their paraphernalia unbearable. He discovers that the other members of the professional staff are terribly busy and seldom around to create a suitable sense of an ongoing academic enterprise. Those who are generally on the premises are not impressed altogether favorably by his dicta about life, art and politics, and, in fact, he may feel his lot to be similar to that of the unfortunate Gilbert and Sullivan policeman—"not a happy one". Under these circumstances, it is difficult to provide the kind of authoritative training in history for architects which is wanted. It is, in fact, the same problem of providing captive specialists that architecture schools face in

---

[18] Ackerman, *op. cit.*, p. 198.
[19] Banham, *op. cit.*, pp. 46-47.

so many areas, from structures and mechanical engineering to materials and equipment.

Because of the need to establish new techniques and more rigorous professional standards in architectural history (notably in language training) there has been great hesitancy about encouraging the kind of hybrid historian-architect who can and will survive and thrive in the professional school milieu. Now, it seems to me, is the time to propose seriously this obvious solution. Fully equipped as a historian, he should be familiar with and sympathetic to the problems of architecture as a profession, as well as interested in its products. He may be a successful or frustrated architect, or not an architect at all, but he should have some sympathy for architecture's creative, intellectual, and technical problems, as well as the usual understanding of its meanings, forms, and social character. What is required is special schooling for the architect or the art historian —preferably a short graduate program for the two together. The training would be designed to make available to the professional schools qualified, creative, and productive architectural historians able to make a contribution of high scholarly caliber to the local educational scene. There is some evidence to indicate that this is not an unreasonable idea.[20]

Fortunately, there has been a retreat from objectivity. Recent commentary suggests that history is not so rigorously scientific as it used to be, although it is still social. There has been some return to the permissive view that so shocked J. A. Froude in 1853 : that history is, after all, literature, an art form in its own right.[21] The inroads of relativism on the old absolutes are made clear in the extraordinary spate of recent books (many of them distinguished) discussing the nature and meaning of history. The old "historicism" whose logic led to such unpleasant extremes, is out of fashion in the west, and there is a general recognition that history, whether literary or not, is made by historians.

---

[20] A pilot program has been undertaken recently at Cornell University. Training leading to the M.A. and Ph.D. degrees is offered in the professional school (College of Architecture) with architectural history as the major subject. This is in addition to the traditional graduate program in the history of art and architecture offered by the Department of History of Art in the College of Arts and Sciences.

[21] Jacques Barzun and Henry F. Graff, *The Modern Researcher.* (New York, 1957). A. L. Rowse, *op. cit.,* p. 77.

Even the Marxist view appears to have softened, and abandoned the old polemic positions. Ernst Fischer, in *The Necessity of Art: a Marxist Approach,* concedes that "the late bourgeois world is still capable of producing art of importance" . . . although "in the long-term view socialist art has the advantage."[22] We can probably afford to accept the view of Karl Popper that "the best institutions can never be foolproof. . . . Institutions are like fortresses. They must be well designed *and* properly manned."[23]

Discussing scientific "progress", Popper goes on to point out that "we can never make sure that the right man will be attracted by scientific research. Nor can we make sure that there will be men of imagination who have the knack of inventing new hypotheses. And, ultimately, much depends on sheer luck, in these matters."[24] The new, more permissive thinking as to what constitutes a valid method and training for architectural history emphasizes a return to the grass roots—to architecture itself—coupled with a sophisticated use of the wide variety methods of investigation now available.[25]

I think most of us would agree with Henry Millon that "it is questionable whether there is any 'true' history . . . History is the selection, organization, and presentation of facts which seem to be most important to the writer. And the process of selection of facts is, in itself, an act of interpretation and will vary from generation to generation." He suggests that too rigid a conception of the historian and his role is self-defeating— that the architectural historian must have free reign in selecting and organizing his material.[26] Under these circumstances, it seems to me, the architectural historian profits greatly from a more direct involvement with architecture than the usual history of art program provides.

Is contemporary architecture a legitimate subject of historical research?

The consciousness of history varies with peoples and times; now

[22] Ernst Fischer, *The Necessity of Art: A Marxist Approach,* trans. Anna Bosetock. (Baltimore, 1963), p. 214.
[23] Karl R. Popper, *The Poverty of Historicism.* (London, 1957), p. 157.
[24] *Ibid.*
[25] Ackerman, *op cit.,* p. 229.
[26] Henry Millon, "History of Architecture, how Useful?" *Journal of the American Institute of Architects,* XXXIV (December 1960), p. 24.

it is dominated by nostalgia for the past, now by the feeling of perservation or hope concerning the future. These fluctuations are easily understood. Certain people expect greatness, others preserve the memory of it, some feel linked with a tradition they wish to prolong, others are eager for novelty, thirsting for liberty and forgetfulness. Time is at once both the destroying power which sweeps into oblivion monuments and empires, and the principle of life and creation. Neither the optimism of progress nor the pessimism of separation and solitude define properly the historical idea.[27]

Contemporary architecture, like any other architecture, is a part of the architectural historian's province. Perhaps the question should be put "can contemporary architecture be the subject of legitimate historical research?" There are special hazards involved in prying into the affairs of the living which are obviated when the people concerned are no longer on the scene, and their ideas and achievements "in the public domain."

Discussion of contemporary work is normally the prerogative of the critic rather than the historian. Few of the facts are as yet recorded, and the social and intellectual milieu are supposed to be known to all. Therefore the historical talents of the architectural historian are not employed in the usual, relatively impersonal way. Rather, he is forced to regard the work in question in terms of the conditions that applied, the goals of the program, and the success of the solution, thus entering into an argument with those who have devoted time, money, effort, or thought to the building and may have a large emotional or financial investment in it. Their careers or profit depend on the kind of impression the building makes. The forces centering around a new building are considerably more powerful and unstable than those involved with old buildings whose place in the community is established and whose amortization is completed. Whether the historian is favorably or unfavorably disposed to the work, he is in trouble. If he is for it, there is always the assumption that he has something to gain—that he has been seduced directly or indirectly. If he is against it, his comment may seem to those whose interests are affected to be malicious or irresponsible. To be absolutely non-committal is difficult, and probably a waste of time. Unless he is prepared to

[27] Raymond Aron, *Introduction to the Philosophy of History: An Essay on the Limits of Historical Objectivity,* trans. George J. Irwin. (London, 1961), p. 319.

produce journalistic criticism (something which more historians should attempt, we are often told) the historian who discusses contemporary architecture in any but the most general way must expect to have the legitimacy of his findings questioned.

There is, however, one important service which architectural historians should perform for contemporary architecture. They should look to their raw material, and attempt to collect and preserve publications and information relating to new structures. Much valuable architectural documentation is ephemeral—brochures, news releases, descriptions, and comment. Unless some individual or agency makes an effort to file this material, it is likely to disappear. Even architectural drawings and renderings of new works are not adequately provided for, and the records of distinguished architects generally die with them. It has long been customary to collect at least samples of materials relating to historic practitioners or projects in school, public, or historical libraries. What is needed are local archives containing significant information about the most recent as well as the oldest buildings of the area. To be of value, such collections must have the expertise and represent the interests of architectural historians.

Do historians influence the development of contemporary architecture?

> The price that historians have had to pay for thus meddling in contemporary affairs has been the debasement of their own stature as purveyors of fact. It is now assumed that an architectural historian writes about a particular subject in the past because he approves of it, or wishes to propagate its renewal.[28]

In April 1961 the *Journal of the Royal Institute of British Architects* reported a session in which England's most indefatigable architectural historian had presented a paper entitled "Modern Architecture and the Historian, or the Return of Historicism."[29] In this Nikolaus Pevsner discussed a series of recent works in architecture which appeared to him to have a suspicious resemblance to seven phases of the avant-garde archi-

---

[28] Banham, *op. cit.*, p. 44.
[29] Nikolaus Pevsner, "Modern Architecture and the Historian, or the Return of Historicism," *Journal, Royal Institute of British Architects*, 3rd series, LXVIII (April 1961), pp. 230-240. The choice of the term "historicism" (as indicated above, often used to indicate a determinist historical view) was unfortunate.

tecture of a half century before—designs which he had brought
to the attention of architecture buffs in *Pioneers of the Modern
Movement,* published in 1936. He accounted for the derivative
nature of the recent efforts as attempts to emulate far-out creative solutions in architecture of the past—that part of the past
not yet old enough to have been imitated in the normal and
traditional eclectic way. The supposition was that these revivals
are attempts to rival the somewhat baroque inventions of the
form-givers of our day. This seems a plausible enough historical
interpretation, but obviously it left in Professor Pevsner's mind
a rather disagreeable sense of having been in some way responsible for these aberrations. He wondered whether he, as the
provider of the necessary documents, was not in some manner
an accessory to the crime of plagiarism committed by the architects in question.

Unless he was flattering himself unduly, Dr. Pevsner had
presented evidence that historians do, in fact, have influence
on the development of contemporary architecture. A sobering
thought. Evidently the coming of what used to be referred to as
"Modern Architecture" a generation ago, with its anti-historical
machine-age aesthetic, was not as purgative as right-thinkers had
happily assumed. The naughty use of architectural history as
an eclectic grab-bag for design scraps was supposed to have
been done away with. But look—here is the old enemy within
the gates, brandishing "neo-de Stijl" in place of neo-classic,
and "neo-German Expressionism" in place of Gothic Revival.
What this suggests is that significant numbers of contemporary
architects have the same attitudes and failings as their Victorian
forbears. In my opinion, we architectural historians are largely
to blame.

It is true that the reverend gentlemen who are now the Old
Masters of architecture attempted to transcend the habitual, the
outmoded, and the ready-made design elements they inherited.
In several senses they made a production out of architecture. In
this they were aided and abetted by gifted historians, in whose
front rank Nikolaus Pevsner surely finds his place. Perhaps
because of their conviction that architectural innovators are
using the forms and expression first developed in painting and
sculpture, historians continued to regard buildings as discrete
phenomena, visual objects with no real context. Reinforced by

technocratic concerns for mass production in building and by the steamship aesthetic that floated so many white "International Style" flying-bridge boxes on such a wide variety of sites throughout the world, they inadvertently continued the Victorian tradition of the "architectral example." New museum pieces were selected and displayed as trophies for the edification and delectation of all observers with pretensions to culture. It is our penchant for isolating the specimen and displaying it handsomely all by itself in order to develop generalities about style or whatever which links us to the age of exploitation.

This kind of exposition encourages the chaotic character of our communities and develops competitive attitudes in consumers and producers alike. Because of our concentration on individual building items we have failed to reckon adequately with the many unrelated or unorganized architectural elements crowding in upon the scene. We have only to compare a photograph of a monumental urban building taken 100 years ago with a photograph taken in our day to see how drastically uncoordinated innovation has affected the community and its architectural expression. What is needed is history of architecture which is meaningful at home, in the ordinary community and situation, rather than the traditional emphasis on the high spots for those who can make the grand tour, either in person or vicariously through slide lectures and picture books. We must have history which emphasizes continuities of regional tradition and the special problems and solutions of particular climatological areas. In addition to the necessary concentration on nuances of the modification of the Miesian prism, or the mirages and ladyfingers of Ronchamp, we must insist on study of the cumulative aspects of historic development, seeing the ways in which a variety of historic forms have been harmonized or contrasted in the past. We must encourage architects and students to see that the world is not, in fact, made up of pieces of blank paper with lines around "plots" on which they can establish their sculptural building masses freely, as though in the remotest desert or the architectural press. We must constantly strive to make them aware of the real artistic and expressive potential of real sites and situations, and of real life. When architects and their public develop a sense of the identity of place and the significance of their time; when they are better aware of which architectural and natural elements already on the scene have design, social, and economic value; when architectural language becomes sufficiently sophisticated for the proper role of quotations or stock items in design to be established, we will know that historans are having a salutary influence on the development of contemporary architecture.

History as an element in shaping the future

> Human life is dialectic, that is, dramatic, since it is active in an incoherent world, is committed despite duration, and seeks a fleeting truth, with no other certainty but a fragmentary science and a formal reflection.[30]

Wherever architectural history has been taught to architects it has directly affected the architecture of the day. While historians do not create new forms, they frequently revive old ones and from the wide range of recorded architectural solutions can select those which seem most attractive or meaningful. To the extent that the historians' formulations are compelling or timely they will become part of the baggage of the architect, serving as data for his design decisions. Affecting both the conscious and the subconscious operations of the designer, historical information is perhaps the most important single resource shaping the architecture of the future.[31]

Since even historians of architecture are not omniscient and cannot divine the future, they must take a broad view of their responsibilities. They must see to it that both architects and "tastemakers"—the influential laymen—have sufficient information and experience in architectural matters to make wise decisions when modifying our environment. Not only must historical indoctrination provide a large fund of knowledge—of facts, impressions, and appreciations of existing large-scale social artifacts—but it must also provide an adequate exposure to the range of ideas, aesthetic effects, technical solutions, social formulations, and specialized traditions which form our architectural heritage. When our designers and their public have a

---

[30] Aron, *op. cit.,* p. 347.

[31] Dr. Banham and other educators now report that both students and historians have noticed (with some embarrassment) that the organized presentation of history of architecture material to student architects is often more effective than time-consuming studio training in developing design insight and organizational skill.

better understanding of the visual and social context in which new designs must find their place—perhaps contrasting, perhaps conforming, but consciously capitalizing on perceptible circumstance—we can expect architecture of historical and human value to appear. History will, in fact, have provided orientation.

ARCHITECTURE AND TRADITION THAT ISN'T "TRAD, DAD"*

Stanford Anderson

Traditionalism, in the sense of seeking to maintain the status quo, has been traditionally, and rightly, combatted by most twentieth-century architects. But, having rejected the authority of tradition, modern architects have then sought a new authority. Most commonly, architects have claimed to find that authority in science or technology. To cite a recent example of such theorising, Dr. Reyner Banham argues that technology "represents the converse of tradition", warns architects to throw themselves wholeheartedly into technology—or else, and summarizes his position as follows: "For the first time in history the world of *what is* is suddenly torn by the discovery that *what could be* is no longer dependent on *what was*."[1]

Between the extremes of traditionalistic "tombstone polishing" and a "compulsive progressivist reflex," the present paper seeks to establish an interpretation of tradition that will recognize our debt to the past without establishing the past as an authority. Furthermore, this paper will encourage a radical adaptation of the methods of scientific discovery with neither the implication of a scientific determinism nor the advocacy of leaping on the latest bandwagon.

I would like to introduce these thoughts in a polemic involving topical attitudes in architecture. I would then like briefly to indicate the epistemological foundation for my position in the work of Professor Karl Popper. Finally, I will propose and

---

*This paper was first presented at a seminar at the Architectural Association, London, in February, 1963.

[1] Reyner Banham, "Architecture after 1960. 1. Stocktaking," *Architectural Review*, CXXVII (February 1960), pp. 93-100, also other articles in this series through June 1960 and, by the same author, "Futurism and Modern Architecture," *Royal Institute of British Architects Journal*, 3rd series, LXIV (February 1957), pp. 129-139; *Theory and Design in the First Machine Age* (London, 1960), especially the last chapter; "The History of the Immediate Future," *R.I.B.A. Journal*, 3rd series, LXVIII (May 1961), pp. 252-260, 269; "Coventry Cathedral—Strictly 'Trad, Dad'," *Architectural Forum*, CXVII (August 1962), pp. 118-119, reprinted from *New Statesman*, LXIII (May 25, 1962), pp. 768-769.

illustrate my resolution of the apparently conflicting claims of science and tradition on architecture by means of an extension of Popper's theory of knowledge.

I. TRADITION VERSUS SCIENCE?

Anti-traditionalism has been virtually a universal characteristic of modern architects. The Futurists expressed most vehemently the not uncommon attitude that the rejection of tradition*ism* implied the rejection of tradition itself—what Banham has referred to as discarding "the whole of our cultural load."[2] The excesses brought about by the mental disease of traditionalism are to be ended by cultural euthanasia rather than by a revised attitude to tradition. I have chosen to introduce my argument through the writing of Reyner Banham for several reasons. Banham makes articulate a view which I believe is implicitly held by many architects. His writings have recently been topical; and thus a summary of them should give perspective to my own position. Finally, I hope that this polemicizing tactic will assure me at least one interested, and interesting, critic.

As aerodynamic theory must change when one reaches the speed of sound, so, according to Banham, "history too has these points of transformation, when a quantitative change becomes a qualitative one."[3] The advent of modern architecture represents for Banham such a qualitative change. The relation of architecture to "its grand traditions, extending from the Pyramids to the Crystal Palace, has clearly been broken for good; it cannot hope to regain its Vitruvian innocence."[4] That is, architecture cannot hope to regain its role as the master technology. Any working tradition—"operational lore"—brought forward from that closed epoch is interpreted by Banham as being based on vague sentiment and in contradiction to the dictates of technology.[5] Nevertheless, as a historian and critic, Banham is happy to acknowledge tradition within the Modern Movement itself; he points out that the architectural phenomenon in Italy known as "Neoliberty" shows "that the allegedly anti-traditional Modern Movement has a tradition of its own."[6]

---

[2] *Theory and Design . . .*, pp. 12 and 329-330.
[3] "The History of the Immediate Future," p. 252.
[4] *Architectural Review*, May 1960, p. 332.
[5] *Ibid.*, February 1960, p. 95.
[6] *Ibid.*, p. 97.

Banham sees the greatest difficulty in deciding what attitude the architect and historian should adopt toward this newfound tradition. He treats "Neoliberty" as a *revival*, and thus it can be condemned. The inclusion of traditional reference in English "New Brutalism" demands from him a more detailed interpretation; for these works may evidence a knowing reuse of some legitimate device or idea from tradition, which he defines as the all-inclusive, "immutable and scientifically ascertainable succession of historical facts."[7] The historian, however, must do more than scientifically ascertain that immutable succession of historical facts; he must also serve as a psychiatrist to the Modern Movement. Banham goes still further to say that: "Without the ballast of an equivalent millenial tradition, architecture will have to be consciously trimmed and steered as it proceeds, and someone will have to plot its course continually. That someone is the historian."[8] Banham appends a statement in which he says that it is not the historian's job to give orders or indicate destinations. But the helmsman can, even unintentionally, run the ship aground despite the best of orders from the bridge. The historian's job of plotting, trimming, and steering is obviously a fateful job. And who, then, is on the bridge giving orders and indicating destinations? Science. Banham sums up his article on tradition with: "This, finally, brings us to the most significant aspect of the rigorous scrutiny of the history of the modern movement: the rediscovery of science as a dynamic force, rather than the humble servant of architecture. The original idea of the early years of the century, of science as an unavoidable directive to progress and development, has been reversed by those who cheer for history, and has been watered down to a limited partnership by the mainstream. Those who have re-explored the Twenties and read the Futurists for themselves feel once more the compulsions of science, the need to take a firm grip on it, and to stay with it whatever the consequences."[9] The latest science to stay with is the "New Biology,"

[7] *Ibid.*, p. 98.
[8] *Ibid.*, May 1960, p. 332. See also Banham's depiction of the historian's job as that of extrapolating the events of the near future from his graph of the past: "The History of the Immediate Future," p. 252.
[9] *Ibid.*, February 1960, p. 99.

because it "looks likely to replace Physics as the master-technology of the mind."[10]

The main points of Banham's position that I want to call into question are the following: Even if we were to accept that such a thing as a qualitative change distinguished modern architecture from that which preceded it, does this liberate us from the past? Is the traditional operational lore of architecture categorically superseded? Or is the situation of architecture similar to that of physics, where older hypotheses—Democritean atomism or Newtonian physics, for example—remain theoretically suggestive or pragmatically operative? But even if we were to acknowledge only the tradition of the Modern Movement itself, what should be our attitude toward tradition? Quite aside from the point that, at best, the writing of history falls somewhat short of achieving an "immutable and scientifically ascertainable succession of historical facts," can historians project a future course? Are tradition and technology hostile opposites which cannot work in concert? Is the concept of a "scientific surf-ride"[11] which demands little more from the architect than daring and a sense of balance the most rational or, indeed, the most radical possible adaptation of science by architecture?

Influence of tradition on modern architecture

Banham prescribes his course of scientific determinism as the means of exorcising the influence of tradition which he documents in his study of *Theory and Design in the First Machine Age*. In this work of charting the recent past of architecture, Banham provides us with much valuable information and many new insights. The book ends with an excellent analysis of the influence of tradition upon the most renowned modern architects, Walter Gropius, Mies van der Rohe, and Le Corbusier. That Banham believes this influence of tradition to be wholly detrimental and contrary to the dictates of technology is apparent from his prophetic and programmatic final paragraph—his own rather inscrutable extrapolation from the historical study which it concludes: "It may well be that what we have hitherto understood as architecture, and what we are beginning to understand of technology are incompatible disciplines. The

[10] "The History of the Immediate Future," p. 257.
[11] *Architectural Review*, June 1960, p. 388.

architect who proposes to run with technology knows now that he will be in fast company, and that, in order to keep up, he may have to emulate the Futurists and discard his whole cultural load, including the professional garments by which he is recognized as an architect. If on the other hand, he decides not to do this, he may find that a technological culture has decided to go on without him. It is a choice that the masters of the Twenties failed to observe until they had made it by accident, but it is the kind of accident that architecture may not survive a second time—we may believe that the architects of the First Machine Age were wrong, but we in the Second Machine Age have no reason yet to be superior about them."[12] Because we are slightly removed from them in time, it is easier for us today to assess the influence of tradition on the architects of the first decades of the twentieth century. From a historical, critical analysis such as Banham's we can recognize pitfalls which we may endeavor to avoid. However, it is pointless to use the critical insights given to us by our fortuitous hindsight as a means of depreciating our predecessors. Rather, these critical insights into the coercive quality of tradition should provide us with information and conjectures which may increase our awareness of our own opportunities. If we have any ground for browbeating the architects of the twentieth century, that ground would not be the universal circumstance that they were influenced by the traditions in which they found themselves. The charge against these architects would rather be the frequency of their self-righteous belief in their independence from tradition. This supposed independence often led them into a blind submission to traditions which they might otherwise have critically observed and overthrown. The conclusion to be drawn from the tradition-bound character of our most famous contemporary architects is not that we must be rid of tradition, but rather that we should acquaint ourselves with our traditions—in order that we may use those traditions more eloquently or free ourselves from them, as we see fit. At times, traditions may be kept vital and more richly and subtly expressive by only the smallest of adjustments or innovations. Again, if our traditions have sunk

---

[12] *Theory and Design* . . ., pp. 329-330. ("Cultural load" is, ironically, misprinted as "cultural lead" on p. 12.)

to the level of torpid convention, radical innovation may be necessary.

Tradition as a common operational ground

The point of the present paper is to suggest that tradition is a necessary, common dynamic ground upon which we operate. When we do assess a part of our tradition as being tyrannical or, on the other hand, ineffectual, it is still only with considerable difficulty that we are capable of discarding even relatively circumscribed parts of that tradition. This difficulty then implies that our best means for realizing our opportunities and for establishing and fulfilling our goals—even radically new goals— is through an acute understanding of our tradition and of its influence upon us.

In seeking to give tradition its appropriate place in our thinking, I do not want to advocate any form of what is usually referred to as "traditionalism". I would not support Coventry Cathedral against Banham's statement that it is "strictly 'trad, Dad.' "[13] It is true that one can understand much about Coventry Cathedral by reference to a whole complex of traditions that are currently operative. But the just criticism that Banham levelled against the clergymen and architects of Coventry Cathedral is precisely that they did not criticize the tradition of cathedral building strongly enough. Such a critique might have found the ancient traditions sufficiently resistant to criticism that one would have avoided compromising them; or it might have found those traditions so susceptible to criticism that the result would have been a radically new architectural form, or no cathedral at all. But the result would hardly have been the "ring-a-ding God-box" that now exists. Writing in this article as a critic rather than as a theoretician, Banham comes very close to the position advocated in the current paper.

Furthermore, I do not want to reinstate the "academic tradition." The implication behind Banham's opposition of "Futurist dynamism" to "Academic caution"[14] is that we must abandon ourselves to the excitement of a blind technological determinism instead of acting according to a complex of factors in our society. Such determinism implies that technology has a

---

[13] "Coventry Cathedral . . . "
[14] *Theory and Design . . .*, p. 12, and chapter 22.

kind of mystic, unconscious will, or that it is at least a closed system which generates its own goals. The influence of extra-scientific, social or governmental decisions on the course of scientific research is well known. The still more obvious influence of external factors upon technology demonstrates that even the proposed authority of technology would not provide independent criteria for action. I accept Professor Popper's non-absolutist analysis of society which denies that there are any independent criteria, or that there is an absolute authority or dogma which can serve as the basis of our actions. The advocacy of this paper is that a critical understanding of our tradition is a necessary aspect of any rational and fruitful context for decision-making.

In this first section, I have tried to suggest the pertinence of my theme to the field of architecture and to forestall any misdirected criticism that would see my paper as a contribution to the shoring up of the Establishment. I would now like to turn to a more systematic presentation of my position.

II. TRADITION AND THE EPISTEMOLOGY OF SCIENCE

The foundation and the superstructure of my argument are to be found in the writings of Karl Popper.[15] In this essay, I can only briefly suggest a few aspects of Popper's theory of knowledge.

The recognition that we make mistakes implies that the quest for certainty is a mistaken quest. We do not ever *know*. We guess; often we learn that our guess is mistaken and that we must abandon or reformulate that guess, giving careful consideration to the way in which our earlier formulation proved to be mistaken. In Popper's words: *"Thus we can learn from our mistakes.* This fundamental insight is, indeed, the basis of all epistemology and methodology: for it gives us a hint how to learn more systematically, how to advance more quickly (not necessarily in the interests of technology; for each individual seeker after truth, the problem of how to hasten one's advance

---

[15] Karl R. Popper, *The Poverty of Historicism* (London, 1957), *The Logic of Scientific Discovery* (London, 1959), *The Open Society and Its Enemies* (London, 4th edition, 1962), *Conjectures and Refutations* (London, 1963). The essay mentioned in note 20, below, published in the last-mentioned volume, will serve as an excellent introduction to the thought of Karl Popper. I would like to express my appreciation to Professor P. K. Feyerabend, who introduced me to Popper's writings at the University of California, Berkeley, in the fall of 1958.

is most urgent). This hint, very simply, is that *we must search for our mistakes*—or in other words, that *we must try to criticize our theories*. Criticism, it seems, is the only way we have of detecting our mistakes, and of learning from them in a systematic way."[16]

What we call "science" is differentiated from other guesses not by being something distinct from other guesses but by the attitude of scientists toward their guesses. They maintain an active critical, or argumentative attitude toward their guesses. With such an attitude one's guesses change in the direction of an ever better account of that which we can observe; that is, our guesses serve to explain the world. Furthermore, such guesses or theories lead us to observe things which we would not otherwise have observed; that is, our theories are predictive. By checking the correspondence of our predictions with our observations, we are able to test our theories. Thus theories serve us for explanation, prediction and testing.

There is no authoritative source for our guesses; we can accept for consideration hypotheses or ideas from any source. The most important problem is how to improve our guesses. The very tradition of problems and hypotheses within one branch of science stimulates criticism and new ventures in that science. But criticism or competing hypotheses may also come from many other quarters; for example, ancient philosophy, science fiction, or other branches of science. It is not at all inconceivable that nuclear physics should find new ideas in biology highly suggestive. But even if we can assume that biology is, as Banham suggests, the most exciting field in science today, we would, nevertheless, be very surprised to see nuclear physics dropping the tradition and logic of its own problem situation and attempting to ride the cresting wave of biology. The provocative ideas of biology would have to be translated into the problem situation of nuclear physics, and then be subjected to the usual severity of testing.

The Futurists did want to ride the waves of a turbulent and exciting body called "science". As earlier artists derived symbolic and aesthetic stimuli from antique myth or from Christianity, and as certain contemporary artists were stimulated by

---

[16] *The Open Society . . .*, addendum, section 5, "Fallibilism and the Growth of Knowledge," pp. 375-376.

primitive art and myth, so the Futurists founded their aesthetic on the excitement which they felt for science and technology. In each case, external stimuli are incorporated into certain artistic traditions. The Futurists too retained traditional artistic mediums such as poetry, painting, sculpture, and architecture. Sant'Elia's earlier work evidences formal influences from the contemporary suburban houses of Paris, from the *Sezessionstil* of Vienna, and perhaps also from Mackintosh and Frank Lloyd Wright. Some of his later monumental projects differ decisively from the slightly earlier romantic visions of an architect like Anasagasti only by Sant'Elia's rigorous omission of academic detail and his gradual introduction of cannons as operative architectural features. The project for which Sant'Elia is most justly renowned, his *città nuova,* is an instance in which Sant'-Elia very inventively posed a problem which had already begun to trouble the Milan of his day—the drastic impingement of the new means of mass transportation on the old concepts and forms of the city. This is to involve one's self in the problem. Especially in an applied art such as architecture, it would be far more radical—if more arduous and less thrilling than surfboarding—to get in and swim. If we were to take a firm grip on theoretical biology and stay with it whatever the consequences, we might, with talent, become theoretical biologists—an excellent consequence unless we had set ourselves the architect's problem of shaping and re-shaping our physical environment. The radical step would be to formulate problems and hypotheses within our own architectural problem situation, and then to criticize and test them as rigorously as our current information and methods permit. As science and technology have been known to profit from science fiction, so architecture could profit from a form of "architectural fiction." But architects must learn not to take such writings and projects as either predictive history or as established theory. Like science fiction, it would bear fruit only when it had been critically assimilated into the problem situation.

There are numerous aspects of architecture that could be investigated as problems in applied science. Such investigations, however, might often be at an even greater remove from the theoretical sciences than are the researches of those disciplines which we recognize as applied sciences. Architects could profit from working with sociologists, though they often would do well to approach sociological problems through the discipline of city planning. Architects might also work with psychologists, biologists, and other scientists; but here too one might often best operate through such applied sciences as acoustics, medicine, etc. A better understanding of the function and testing of theory in the theoretical and applied sciences, and of the way in which these sciences relate to architecture could help us to state our problems and improve our conjectures much more systematically and meaningfully.

In contrast to the practical, predictive use of theory by the applied sciences, the theoretical or generalizing sciences are interested in the theories themselves—in the truth of these theories and consequently in testing them. But among these generalizing sciences, the accuracy of prediction, explanation and testing varies; for example, contrast sociology with physics. Universal theory in sociology has in some way to subsume the eccentricities and independence of human actions, conflicting moral and ethical codes, etc., whereas physical theory is concerned with the comparatively regular phenomena of matter and motion. Or to put it another way, in sociology, tradition becomes a constituent part of scientific, or at least of semi-scientific, theory. The social sciences are intended to study tradition rationally; and "a theory of tradition must be a sociological theory, because tradition is obviously a social phenomenon".[17]

A theory of tradition

Popper has proposed a preliminary theory of tradition. He posits that a kind of proto-theoretical "horizon of expectations" is innate in man, as in other animals. Experience requires the adjustment of these expectations. Popper sees the origin and propagation of tradition in man's need to introduce structure and regularity into his natural and social environment. For our individual well-being, and for the opportunity to concentrate and direct our energies, we require a certain predictability of our environment and of our fellow man. Our social life is only possible when we can have confidence that certain aspects of our society must be or act in this wise and not otherwise. Out of these needs traditions arise.

---

[17] "Towards a Rational Theory of Tradition," in *Conjectures . . .*, p. 123.

But these necessary functions which traditions fulfill—explanation and prediction—are, we should note, the functions of theories. Traditions play a role similar to theories. "Just as the invention of myths or theories in the field of natural science has a function—that of helping us to bring order into the events of nature—so has the creation of traditions in the field of society."[18] And in this role of theory, traditions give us something upon which to operate—a means of communication (including, but not restricted to, language) and a body of conventional usages and ideas which are, nevertheless, subject to criticism and change. Similar to science, society proceeds by the tradition of changing its traditional myths. But this process implies the impossibility of starting with a *tabula rasa*. To use Popper's words, "blue prints have no meaning except in a setting of traditions and institutions—such as myths, poetry, and values —which all emerge from the social world in which we live. . . . You may create a new theory, but the new theory is created in order to solve those problems which the old theory did not solve."[19] Thus tradition serves as the ground of our thoughts and actions. "Quantitatively and qualitatively by far the most important source of our knowledge—apart from inborn knowledge—is tradition. Most things we know we have learned by example, by being told, by reading books, by learning how to criticize, how to take and accept criticism, how to respect truth."[20]

In propounding this theory of tradition, one should also, perhaps, point out what the theory does not support. Although the theory sees the denial of the importance and influence of tradition as futile, it does not support conventional traditionalism. There is no hallowing of any thing or event simply because it occurred in the past. Tradition *per se* has no authority. On the contrary, every aspect of our tradition is open to criticism and rejection. This implies that the tradition we prize is not a mere

---

[18] *Ibid.*, p. 131. Popper's phrase "creation of traditions" is perhaps not the most felicitous. Just as the scientist invents a new theory, but must see that the scientific community accepts it before it is effective, so also in social or cultural matters one invents a new theory or a new way of doing things but must await more general acceptance before it is "traditional." Thus "creation of traditions" appears to oversimplify the situation.

[19] *Ibid.*, p. 132.

[20] "On the Sources of Knowledge and of Ignorance," in *Conjectures* . . . , section xvi 4, pp. 27-28.

accumulation of knowledge, an undifferentiated catalog of past events, but rather a vital body of ideas, values, mores, and so forth that we have as yet found resistant to criticism. Finally, the critical attitude toward tradition permits us to acknowledge the unrelenting influence of tradition upon us without viewing it as an irrational cosmic force which we can only accept. Popper has characterized conventional traditionalism "as the belief that, in the absence of an objective and discernible truth, we are faced with the choice between accepting the authority of tradition, and chaos; while rationalism has, of course, always claimed the right of reason and of empirical science to criticize, and to reject, any tradition, and any authority, as being based on sheer unreason or prejudice or accident."[21]

III. ARCHITECTURE AND THE EPISTEMOLOGY OF SCIENCE

Since Popper's theory of knowledge is a general theory and has been extended by him to a sociological theory of tradition, it is plausible to seek to extend his ideas further to non-scientific fields—including the arts.[22] The most serious apparent, though perhaps not insuperable, shortcoming is that the arts seem to have no coherent set of generally accepted theories or universal laws. However, since art does form part of our social situation, one may explore the interpretation of the arts within a sociological theory of tradition. Furthermore, one may study the relationship of the arts to traditions within the arts themselves; that is, the formal, technical and iconographic traditions. Interest in these methods of the study of the arts developed independently of any deduction from Popper's theory of knowledge. The studies by Professor Gombrich, of the interaction of both the broader and the more confined traditions with the arts of painting and sculpture, represent a most impressive confluence of these several scholarly traditions.[23]

Architecture and tradition

In arguing the unrelenting influence of tradition, one need

---

[21] *Ibid.,* p. 6.
[22] Cf. W. W. Bartley III, *The Retreat to Commitment* (New York, 1962), and numerous other studies listed in note 7, p. 157 of Bartley's book.
[23] E. H. Gombrich, *Art and Scholarship* (London, 1957), *Art and Illusion* (New York, 2nd edition, 1961), "Tradition and Expression in Western Still Life," *Burlington Magazine*, CIII (May 1961), pp. 175-180, "Art and the Language of Emotions," *Proceedings of the Aristotelian Society*, supp. vol. XXXVI (1962) pp. 215-234, and *Meditations on a Hobby Horse* (London, 1963), a collection of essays which includes the first and third entries in this note.

not comment on the incidence of works of art that obviously stand in a particular tradition. It can be acknowledged that in some of such works tradition may have exerted an irrational and unwanted influence; it is for that reason that we must criticize our tradition. Nevertheless, the most treacherous impact of tradition is upon those who seek to escape their tradition, rather than to acknowledge, and reshape it. Consequently, works by artists who seek to escape tradition, or works that are popularly interpreted as tradition-defying, have a peculiar interest.

An inverted form of escape from tradition is literal revivalism —revivalism that is not critical of that which it seeks to revive. In architecture, one thinks, for example, of Pugin's version of Gothic revival as contrasted to the more limited and critical Gothicism of Viollet-le-Duc. More interesting still is the relationship of apparently novel works to tradition. The search for novelty is a major aspect of art that Professor Gombrich has acutely analyzed.[24]

I would like briefly to survey these two types of escapism— literal and uncritical revivalism, and the search for utter novelty. The literal revivalism of Pugin is evidenced in his famous book, *Contrasts,*[25] in which he emphasized what he was not alone in considering the low state of nineteenth-century architecture by contrasting it with medieval examples.

Uncritical revivalism: Pugin in the nineteenth century, despite himself

In the second edition of his book, Pugin was prepared to admit that his earlier formulation—that Protestantism had led to degeneracy in architecture—was inadequate. Rather, it was, he said, the decayed state of faith throughout Europe in the fifteenth century that "led men to dislike, and ultimately forsake, the principles and architecture which originated in the self-denying Catholic principle, and admire and adopt the luxurious styles of ancient Paganism."[26] The resurgence of "good" architecture would not be possible within the live traditions of the nineteenth century. Rather, such a resurgence was dependent

---

[24] "Tradition and Expression . . ."

[25] A. W. N. Pugin, *Contrasts, or a Parallel between the noble Edifices of the fourteenth and fifteenth Centuries and similar Buildings of the present Day* (London, 1836, 2nd edition, 1841).

[26] *Contrasts,* 2nd edition, p. iii; wherever used, the italics are Pugin's.

on a fundamental change in man's world view—on the revival of commitment to a particular body of religious dogma. Pugin was shocked that even some wealthy British Catholics would not support the revival of "pointed architecture": "Some apparently reject tradition and authority,"[27] he said with indignation. It is this union of tradition *and* authority that leads to quixotic, if not to even more desperate events. But Pugin was not unaware that his revival of medieval architecture would suffer some delay if he were to await the complete change of his social milieu. Thus it appears in his writings that the re-commitment of the artist alone will suffice to bring about the desired revival. "The student of Christian architecture should also imbue his mind with the mysteries of the Faith, the history of the Church, the lives of the glorious Saints and Martyrs. . . . He should also be well acquainted with the annals of his country—its constitutions, laws, privileges, and dignities . . . *for we do not wish to produce mere servile imitators of former excellence of any kind, but men imbued with the consistent spirit of the ancient architects, who would work on their principles, and carry them out as the old men would have done, had they been placed in similar circumstances, and with similar wants to ourselves.*"[28]

The influence of the live tradition is implicit in this last statement; that even Pugin could hope for no more than the introduction of a foreign element into that live tradition appears to be explicit in the following defense against critics who thought that Pugin should have put the nineteenth century in a more favorable light by contrasting "pointed style" buildings with those of the Middle Ages: "This objection," Pugin said, "may be answered in a few words: revivals of ancient architecture, although erected *in*, are not buildings of, the nineteenth century—their merit must be referred back to the period from whence they were copied; the architecture of the nineteenth century is that extraordinary conglomeration of classic and modern styles peculiar to the day, and of which we can find no example in any antecedent period."[29] One need not condemn Pugin's dissatisfaction with the extraordinary conglomeration that was the extant, if rather benighted, architectural tradition of the

---

[27] Pugin, *An Apology for the Revival of Christian Architecture in England* (London, 1843), p. 24.
[28] *Ibid.*, pp. 21-22.
[29] *Contrasts*, 2nd edition, p. v.

nineteenth century. But the ease with which we distinguish
Gothic Revival from Gothic architecture is evidence that a style
from the past could not be artificially re-established without
evidencing that artificiality. Perhaps even Pugin's unwillingness
to contrast the "pointed style" with the Gothic was an acknowl-
edgment that at best he had complicated the extraordinary
conglomeration of styles peculiar to the day.

Thus Pugin's ideal was the revival of true Catholic principle
in at least some architects and, to whatever degree possible, in
society at large. The result would be good, Pointed architecture,
the merit of which would have to be referred back to the middle
ages. Pugin hoped that this all-of-a-piece revivalism would lift
one right out of any compromise with contemporary traditions.
What this escapist attitude actually meant was that Pugin was
not at all in a position to deal with the evils of the contemporary
tradition; his anachronistic endeavors would not challenge the
most pressing problems directly and could not provide the
innovation necessary to transform the condition of architecture.
The reverse happened; the condition of architecture in nineteenth century England transformed Pugin's anachronisms into
another variation on its own theme.

By the end of the century, dissatisfaction with extraordinary
conglomerations was widespread. Virtually all the younger
artists agreed that the social body, or at least the body of the
arts, was sick. The diagnoses and the proposed cures were extremely various; but as radical as some of the prescriptions were,
even the anthroposophist and Nietzschean faith-healers were
involved with current traditions. Perhaps its convalescent character was all that unified this early modern architecture; but
even with their frequently categorical over-simplification of the
problem, or over-statement of the proposed solution, these endeavors had at least the potential of being criticizable conjectures about the condition and possible improvement of architecture. It was various aspects of this tradition that led, for
example, to the Deutscher Werkbund, the Bauhaus, and the
International Style—movements which incurred Banham's criticism for evidencing the influence of tradition.

Futurism, tradition and innovation
Even in the radical days of the early part of this century,

however, few people diagnosed the case of society as incurable and proposed cultural euthanasia. Even when the Futurists did propose discarding our cultural load in favor of novelty, it was clear that this anti-traditionalism—as Professor Gombrich has demonstrated in the other arts—required a tradition against which to rebel. As Pugin sought to remove himself from the contemporary problem situation by complete withdrawal to an earlier position, so the Futurists sought to achieve the same removal by stepping into the future. But their future was in large part negatively defined. Tradition at least established what the Futurists purposed not to do; for example, the interdiction on the painting of the nude. Even the Futurist manifestos were not devoid of traditional influence, as Banham himself has demonstrated.[30]

For all the Futurist protestations against monumentality and weightiness, Sant'Elia's freest flights of fancy are peculiarly monumental and weighty. When Sant'Elia did not seek to be so free, when he consciously attempted the critique of a problem—as in the *città nuova* designs—his work was both more inventive and more contributive. Even today these designs startle us because they inventively exceed our expectations; continued exposure reveals the comprehensibility and ingenuity of these designs. From whatever source, we may most heartily welcome innovation which comes to bear upon a carefully conceived problem situation. But sheer novelty would not communicate to us; indeed, it can well be argued that a "novel" situation would not be observed by us unless it were somehow seen in a context we already understood.

Conjecture and criticism in architecture

In architecture, in the twentieth century, we have not lacked for conjectures, nor for criticism. But I would suggest that we have failed to establish a rational attitude toward our conjectures and criticism. What are only conjectures have been put forward as utopian panaceas and supported with absolutist fervour. Corroboration is always sought; never falsification. There are frequent manifestos of what is manifestly unmanifest.

---

[30] Banham, "Sant'Elia," *Architectural Review*, CXVII (May 1955), pp. 295-301, "Footnotes to Sant'Elia," *ibid.*, CXIX (June 1956), pp. 343-344, "Futurism . . .," *op. cit.*, "Futurist Manifesto," *Architectural Review*, CXXVI (August-September 1959), pp. 77-80, *Theory and Design . . .*, section 2.

This absolutist attitude encourages personal criticism against the author rather than rational criticism of the conjecture.

Only when we take a more critical attitude toward our conjectures shall we be able rationally to support, or reject, some of those ideas which currently operate according to the dictates of taste and fashion. With other conjectures, we may be able to define the limits within which they operate. The revised adoption of such traditional "operational lore" as arithmetical number patterns may yet prove to be *technologically* rewarding in the modular co-ordination of industrialized building products. And an example of the efficacy of even *ad hoc* criticism is the development of public housing. The dense, dark packing of inadequate dwellings behind pompous façades in the Berlin *Mietkaserne* of the late nineteenth century; the multiplication of *Existenzminimum* dwelling units into large, orderly blocks during the economy-minded days of the Weimar Republic; the "city-in-a-park" concept of Le Corbusier as partially realized at Roehampton; all these represent conjectures on the solution of the public housing problem. Each of these conjectures has been criticized, though too often according to what Popper has called the "conspiracy theory of society."[31] Even in the case of the *Mietkaserne,* it would be more advantageous to criticize the systems of finance, taxation, and city planning that encourage profit-taking in such ventures rather than to criticize the supposed conspiracy to house people badly. The extent to which Jane Jacobs' attack[32] implies a "conspiracy of ineptness" on the part of modern planners, makes her criticism an exaggerated prodding. It is specific ineptitudes within the problem situation that we must criticize; not a fictional conspiracy to be inept. Despite only rather *ad hoc* criticism, I think we would agree that public housing has improved during the century. Park Hill, Sheffield, is now an excellent conjecture which hopes to resolve some of the problems which earlier developments left open to criticism. We may hope to learn all the more from Park Hill in that it is the subject of continuing sociological study. We learn from the proposal, testing, and reformulation or rejection of simple and apparently inadequate hypotheses such as the *Existenzminimum.* The employment of a greater critical awareness

---

[31] "Towards a Rational Theory of Tradition," in *Conjectures . . .*, p. 123.
[32] Jane Jacobs, *The Death and Life of Great American Cities* (New York, 1961).

during the development of large-scale housing projects which are based on such hypotheses might have provided us with much usable information. Even today, critical, historical and sociological studies of these projects could prove highly instructive concerning the limits within which these conjectures may be valid, or at least concerning the ways in which they failed to solve their problems. In other words, such studies could suggest a redefinition of the problems and, thereby, new conjectures as well.

Advice to students of architecture

Finally, I would like to summarize this advocacy with the suggestion that Professor Popper's proposed advice to students of the sciences could be paraphrased to apply to architects: "Try to learn what people are discussing nowadays in science. Find out where difficulties arise, and take an interest in disagreements. These are the questions which you should take up. In other words, you should study the *problem situation* of the day. This means that you pick up, and try to continue, a line of inquiry which has the whole background of the earlier development of science behind it; you fall in with the tradition of science. It is a very simple and a decisive point, but nevertheless one that is often not sufficiently realized by rationalists—that we cannot start afresh; that we must make use of what people before us have done in science. If we start afresh, then, when we die, we shall be about as far as Adam and Eve were when they died (or, if you prefer, as far as Neanderthal man). In science we want to make progress, and this means that we must stand on the shoulders of our predecessors. We must carry on a certain tradition. From the point of view of what we want as scientists—understanding, prediction, analysis, and so on—the world in which we live is extremely complex. I should be tempted to say that it is infinitely complex, if the phrase had any meaning. We do not know where or how to start our analysis of this world. There is no wisdom to tell us. Even the scientific tradition does not tell us. It only tells us where and how other people started and where they got to. It tells us that people have already constructed in this world a kind of theoretical framework—not perhaps a very good one but one which works more or less; it serves us as a kind of network, or as a system of co-ordinates to which we can refer the various complexities of this world. We use it by checking it over, and by criticizing it. In this way we make progress."[33]

---

[33] "Towards a Rational Theory of Tradition," in *Conjectures* . . ., p. 129.

CONVENIENT BENCHES AND HANDY HOOKS
Functional Considerations in the Criticism of the Art of Architecture

Reyner Banham

I was a bit surprised to be invited to come here to speak *qua criticus* rather than *qua historicus*, because history is, of course, my academic discipline. Criticism is what I do for money. History, however, is fairly congruent in its intentions, and to some extent in its methods, with the view of criticism which I am going to outline this morning.

Those of you who have done your homework and read the summary of my paper will observe that it starts with a quotation from Suzanne Langer. But this is not an anti-Langer diatribe. I happened to come across this quotation at the time when I was putting the paper together, and it struck me that the sentiment which it contained is one that might have come from a number of academic critics or evaluators of the architectural scene. Indeed, it touches on a fairly crucial problem, for she says, "besides the difficulties presented to art theory in general by the good and bad odors of words which interfere with their strict meanings and by the variety of even their defined meaning in literature, each art has its special incubus of natural misconceptions. The affliction of literature is its relation to facts, the affliction of architecture, the obvious fact of utility." The obvious fact of utility has always been one of the stumbling blocks in the critical evaluation of architecture as an art.

Like industrial design but unlike the so-called fine arts—what I would call the portable arts, painting and sculpture—architecture deals with the problem of use as well as, or parallel with, or on top of or underneath, the problem of symbolic expression, or whatever else you would like to call it. This, in the end, is why I involve myself with architecture, rather than any of the other aspects of the creative arts, which as an art historian I might have been expected to go into.

Architecture has this added moral grandeur as well as the embarrassment of being a direct physical service to man as well

91

as an expression of his social, personal and cultural aspirations. I don't think many of us, in fact, could support a mode of criticizing or discussing architecture which regards utility as an affliction, even though we may feel that the particular utility which we have to serve is an affliction on that particular day, with that particular hand or suggestion or whatever is wrong in the office. It is in fact, pretty well impossible to discuss individual buildings in this way. It is impossible to discuss the building without discussing what it is for. Above all, to treat utility as an affliction, as something that should be set on one side in discussing a building, is to leave out the reasons why the building was created in the first place and the performance that society expects of it. If you leave out the fact of utility, you leave out the "why" of architecture as a human activity; yet a great deal of architectural writing appears to (and has to) support this dichotomy of method.

In the situations we find ourselves in at present, we often get pushed into the position of having to proceed as if we accepted this split in method. For one thing, the production of a properly generalized theory of architecture really involves leaving out the particulars. If you are going to begin to generalize, then your final intellectual construct, document or whatever which embodies the theory will have to leave out pretty well all the particulars in order to achieve a general rule. But, presented with a particular building on a particular site, criticism, evaluation, history cannot proceed in the absence of such particulars as the designated function of the building. Practically every critic, practically every historian, practically every journalist who is in the business, in fact, changes gear persistently between the one and the other mode of operation, general and particular.

No doubt there is a question of temperamental preference involved here. When we got back from Lafayette Park the day before yesterday,[1] the response of different people to what we had seen was interestingly polarized. Colin Rowe wanted to discuss the end of the Modern Millenium, but other people wanted to discuss the ends of the mullions. Both saw the after-

---

[1] The members of the seminar had made a bus tour of notable buildings in Detroit and vicinity two days previously.—*Editor.*

noon as a disastrous experience, but the terms of reference in which the disaster was phrased varied in allegiance from the general to the particular. As I say, I think there is a temperament-factor, but I think there is also an operational consideration. It is very *difficult* to work a generalized theory without throwing away a great deal of what is most germane and most essential to a particular building. Now, the inability that we clearly face at the moment, of creating a general theory of criticism, except by leaving out most of the things that make buildings interesting, has led to this feeling that architectural theory has become vacuous and irrelevant. People feel differently about this situation, and Peter Collins is rather shocked that we at the University College in London should have decided we could get along without theory for a bit, because we could find nothing particularly solid or interesting in the category normally labeled "theory." We don't necessarily share Mrs. Moholy's objections to this word "theory," nor do we have that attachment to the idea of theory which is evidenced, I think, by things that Peter Collins has said, or Colin Rowe—that attachment to theory which seems to go with the Beaux-Arts or French kind of architectural formation. Our reasons for being pragmatic about theory are purely pragmatic ones; that we could find very little useful in there that an architect needs or can work with.

Now I must point out that we were talking about theory in (I suspect) the sort of sense which Peter Collins means by it. We were talking about theory dealing with the forms and relationships of the component units of building designs—"Dualities must not be left unresolved" etc. But I am perfectly aware that in a great number of schools and in a great number of traditions of teaching the theory of architecture is not like that at all. The category "theory of architecture" having become vacuous, empty of formal content and devices, has been used as a sort of general purpose carrier-bag or hold-all, into which you stuff sociology, computer programming and anything else which cannot be taught at the drawing board but which you feel architects ought to know. In fact, it struck me that one of the solutions to Mr. Zevi's problem would be to create one chair labeled "architectural theory" which covers all these miscellaneous subjects which people complained about last night; because architectural theory, as it is commonly discussed at the moment, is all those things like sociology and other aspects of useful knowledge which have to be taught and are in fact not theory at all—simply miscellaneous background information that makes an architect a little wiser in the ways of the world and of the kind of social situation in which he will be building. But they are not architectural theory in the sense that academics would prefer to understand it, meaning a body of rules, a body of laws (even if you split the meaning of rule and law in the Louis Kahn manner), rules and laws derived from the observation of the form and functions of buildings. This is not to say that obviously those pretenses to be the principles of teachings do not depend on a body of belief or dogma, as I think it was called yesterday, but that in general nowadays, belief and dogma do not tend to be an organized body of information with some kind of logical scheme; it is much more a question of attitude and temperament.

But the reason why, in the end, the question of theory is felt to be vacuous, is because of the absence of those particular reasons, which cause buildings to be created and cause buildings to be the precise way they are. Architects are committed (at any rate in the Western nations, and the cultures which derive from the European tradition) to a pragmatic position. Architects do *not* begin to operate until someone comes to them with a proposition. Serge Chermayeff may make his crack about architects being ladies of easy virtue who are standing around waiting to be propositioned by a client; but if, indeed, we are professional harlots, then the same is true, of course, of lawyers, doctors, consulting engineers and anybody else whose activity depends upon someone else coming forward with the proposition in one hand and the money bag in the other. The client or person in need of assistance has to come forward to us with a proposal to do a particular thing and then the architect or consultant can join the act to implement the client's desire.

And therefore the kind of proposition made by Suzanne Langer tends to be repugnant to us because it rejects precisely the main springs of architectural creativity, that is, the challenge of the functional program. This is when architecture starts. When Mr. X, Mr. Blandings says, "This is what I would like done," the architect then applies himself to the solution of the particular problem, to produce a design embodying the client's conception of the building's use.

Now, I am using the word program loosely here and I am not excluding any number of different responses to the program. We have had a spate of discussion in England recently of the precise meaning of the program and the architect's proper attitude towards it. John Summerson, in his famous paper at the RIBA on the absence of any theory of modern architecture, spoke of the program as being the generator of architectural form in the modern movement, and subsequently we have had the views of Professor Llewelyn-Davies (and many other people) to the effect that the program, for what it is worth as written by the client and formulated by the client, is a document which the architect is obliged to treat with extreme suspicion, that even in the very vaguest formulation he should read and study the program carefully until he understands it and then tear it up and find out what the client really wants. Whichever of these situations—whether the program is accepted plainly or whether the program is rejected, and reformulated with the client—whichever situation applies, the challenge of the fundamental program is what gets the architect started on the business of designing the building. It is his basic term of reference, and this is the basic term of reference to which the whole discussion of the building must return. Not only the architect's discussion of the building but the critic's discussion of the building must come back in the end in some way to what the architect once thought, or supposed to have been done, or should have been doing in creating the building. Now this is something which many critics are happy to pass up. A great deal of European criticism of the Frank Lloyd Wright's domestic architecture, rather than finding out what Frank Lloyd Wright was supposed to be doing, is happily prepared to suppose that Frank Lloyd Wright was doing what a European architect would be doing in designing a domestic residence. There is plenty of evidence, inside the *Autobiography* and outside of it, that nothing of the sort is true. Much of the criticism which you get from European architects of the wastefulness, disorganization and mechanical inefficiency of Frank Lloyd Wright's planning (some of which may be true; not having lived in a Wright house, I cannot really be certain about this) proceeds on the assumption that Frank Lloyd Wright was designing a bad European house rather than designing a good Chicago or mid-western house.

The knowledge of the original brief or program becomes more and more crucial to the critic's approach to a building, as the building itself becomes less and less formal and susceptible to the rules. A great deal of architecture is still relatively formal and susceptible to the rules and this is especially true of the great mass of domestic architecture created in any one country; what satisfies common needs is not worked out from a particular program but from a formulation of that country's socially acceptable ideas and aspirations. And this is true, whether the house is by Levitt or by Paul Rudolph. In general the revolutionary or unexpected content of domestic architecture is low. Contrariwise, in fields like building for the teaching or practice of scientific studies there is very little that can be said to be formal, ritual or routine about the design, and the critic—or anybody else who happens to try to evaluate it—needs to know the brief in some detail. It may not improve his opinion of the building, but it will at least improve the certainty of what he has to say about it. It is, in fact, becoming increasingly difficult just to look at a building and say usefully what you think about it. We all do look at buildings and say what we think about them. On Wednesday, we all took one look and damned everything we saw.[2] We ought to be ashamed of doing that, as hardly any of us had any detailed knowledge of the background of the buildings, or particularly, of the original brief which the building was supposed to serve.

The position of the original functional brief is, as most of us would allow in our saner moments, vital to an evaluation of a building and contains information too valuable to be missed. But is it essential to the appreciation of the building as a work of art? To go back to Suzanne Langer again, "a virtual environment, the creative space of architecture, is a symbol of functional existence. This does not mean, however, that signs of

<hr>

[2] Another reference to the tour of Detroit architecture made by members of the seminar.—*Editor.*

important activities, hooks for implements, convenient benches, well planned doors, play any part in its significance. In that thought's assumption lies the error of functionalism. Symbolic expression is something miles removed from provident planning or good arrangement."

This must be a very tough thing for most of us to accept. We are all, to some extent, committed to the functionalist's approach which she decries and also, quite simply, there is usually not enough in the budget for utility and symbolic expression to be significantly separated—by the time you finish serving utility, you have awfully little left over to serve symbolic expression.

You will notice in this particular discussion, that she takes an extremely simple or apparently simple example. One has the impression that when she says "hooks for implements, convenient benches, well planned doors" she is deliberately playing it down to primitivism or, at any rate, a kind of Shaker refinement and simplicity in design, rather than taking it at the full blooded level of a rich and culturally affluent society. The actual terms of reference she uses here suggest to me very strongly the traditional Norwegian farm house. Its construction is on the log cabin principle and it has a highly ritualized plan, which persisted in Norway almost to the beginning of this century. The basic plan is something like this. It's a plain log-house form, which I suppose derived naturally from the use of straight pine poles in a structural method. It has only one major subdivision within the rectangle which rules off about one fifth of the floor area at one end. You enter through the front half of this area which forms a place for hanging up your outdoor skins to dry —it rains and rains on the west coast of Norway—so this is for general purposes, for undressing and storing; the dry store of the house is in the back half of the ruled-off area. If it has a second story, it is also purely storage. Coming to the living room, we find that it is furnished in almost exactly the kind of terms that Suzanne Langer is using in that quotation. There are two built-in beds which are backed up against the wall, high box-beds, each with a kind of underground kennel for dogs underneath. At the opposite end to the beds and the entrance there is a built-in bench which runs right across the end-wall. The master's seat is in the middle of the bench and the whole thing is a ritual plan which is almost incapable of variation. Even when the Norwegians became richer and more powerful and more settled (nonetheless still at the mercy of outside interference such as the Swedes and Danes and so forth), they still continued to build this plan, except it got bigger and bigger until you finally find a version where that bench is something like 28 feet long; you need quite a family to fill that, especially as the table which stands against the bench according to ritual also demands a second bench, a movable one which may take four men to lift, on the other side.

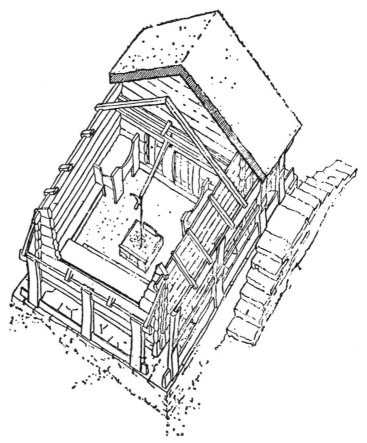

Isometric drawing of a house in the Norsk Folkemuseum. Reproduced from G. Kavli, *Norwegian Architecture Past and Present* (Oslo, 1958).

Thus we have an interior in which utility and the symbolic expression (of agronomic pride, success and so forth) cannot be distinguished. It may be at a low cultural level—I am not disputing that—but the particular quotation from Suzanne Langer that I was using pitches the argument on a fairly fundamental cultural level. But then, into this tight functional and symbolic domain of useful furniture comes one extraordinary random element which is very disturbing the first time you see it. It is a dirty great tree branch which wanders across the middle of the room just above head-level. It has to be a tree branch for purely functional reasons, and for the same reasons, the tree branch has to be attached to part of the trunk. The trunk part is hinged in a couple of wooden straps to one of the big wooden beams which brace the roof-plates, and from the last kink in the branch hangs the cooking pot over the central hearth. You could almost have breakfast in bed because this cooking-crane will swing from over the hearth to the side of the bed.

It is the one element of random geometry (or something other than geometry) which intrudes into this otherwise rigorously geometrical interior. It is for that reason an immensely expressive object, and it is the individualation of that particular household. Thus one could say that when the builder went out to choose a branch for the cooking crane, he had to make both a functional and a symbolic decision about what to use. Here, it seems to me, is an interior (if not a total house) in which the symbolic elements, few and simple as they are, cannot be distinguished from the handy hooks and convenient benches, because they *are* the handy books and convenient benches, there is nothing else to see in that interior. The whole, if it is a "symbol of functional existence," is what the Chicago School of Esthetic Philosophers would call an iconic sign, where the symbol cannot be distinguished from the thing it symbolizes.

But the kind of architecture that we have to criticize, evaluate, understand and teach nowadays is an architecture which is not ritualized. It depends on, we believe, conscious personal choices pretty well right through the process of design. The differences between vernacular and contemporary functional design are, I think, probably even more profound than we commonly allow and certainly cut deep and confusingly through our present processes of criticism. Because we do not trust other people, above all do not trust other architects, we prefer, as often as not, the kind of "anonymous architecture" which is illustrated in Mrs. Moholy's book of the same name. Because we are a tight, jealous and suspicious profession, we really prefer looking at work done not by architects at all (or we like to think they were not done by architects at all). We put an evaluation on "anonymous architecture," the "functional tradition," and so forth, which is far above what is justified by the social and operational situation in which the buildings were created, and quite unlike the situation in which architects now find themselves, in which things will go by complexes of profound and confused decisions often taken in unlikely circumstances. Nevertheless, they are decisions which have been taken.

Now, it is given to very few architects suddenly to see the whole thing in one blinding flash of light, like the conversion of Paul on the way to Damascus. We know that only a very simple or simple-minded kind of building in fact is created in that one simple flash. The crucial decision may in fact be taken in split micro-seconds, but as a consequence of days of torn-up sketches, of arguments, of telephone calls to the client, tantrums, hangovers and that kind of thing. The actual creative moment strikes after days, weeks, sometimes months of contemplation, cogitation and working it over. It is often a long process, it is something which has a history of its own. This is true, even more so, when the process of the design is not the work of a single man. The process may not be personal, it may be so to speak a group history, but it remains equally true that the work of say, the Architects Collaborative or one of the English "systems" teams is even more of a historical process and in fact more easy to lay out as a process, because the decisions and inquiries have to be formulated and transmitted from one man to another. I know it is often said: "Yes, but really, there is *one* person on the team who is the designer." I could in fact point at cases in English practice where no one man is the designer, where, although there may have been leadership and counsel from one man, the final solution of the design cannot be credited to any one single person. There are situations in which the process of design is genuinely collaborative and not in any normal sense individual.

Nevertheless, what I want to put forward is the proposition that the kind of criticism which will work nowadays—one in which one does not get into difficulties over form versus function, or symbolic expression, or whatever—the kind of criticism which will work is what I called in my original notes an existential criticism, but which I probably should have called a situationist criticism. Such criticism, to my mind, should start with the architect confronted with the client's proposition; the situation of the professional man faced with a commission from a client. And the criticism proceeds from there, to write what might almost be called the biography of the man during the time he was committed to doing this, his professional biography as a designer. This may sound a tall order but it has been done at least once recently, though disguised. The method has already been studied, in Professor Jordy's history (or whatever it is) of the Philadelphia Savings Fund Building by Howe and Lescaze.[3] That to me is not only one of the great historical documents of recent years but, because it takes you through the entire decision-making history of the project and identifies the individual contributions of the various specialists, the consequences of the various economic and other pressures, right up to completion date, it is a profound and radical evaluation of the building.

Where does this leave the value judgment aspect of criticism, which doubtless is what criticism is for? Much as one may say that criticism is to explain, to make clear how and why the building has got to be the way it is, evaluation is a very important function at the moment. Particularly, I think, in lay criticism, because the buildings are not formalized and ritualized, now that every building is supposed to be designed as if buildings never existed before. For this reason a great deal must be explained as to how and why the building got to be in the shape it is in. But when there has to be value judgment in what appears to be a purely descriptive process, I think it must emerge from the process itself. This may be a very relativistic position since it might be supposed that you create no values by describing the building. Yet I think the key to the value judgment,

---

[3] W. H. Jordy, "PSFS: Its Development and Its Significance in Modern Architecture," *Journal of the Society of Architectural Historians*, XXI (May 1962), pp. 47-83.

and what justifies the descriptive process, is finding (or failing to find) exemplified in the building, the consistent working out of a personal response to the commission and seeing to what extent it is a consistent and demonstrative (or whatever else you would like to call it) working-out of that particular functional program. Two examples I had in mind were Rudolph's Art and Architecture Building at Yale and Stirling's Engineering Block at Leicester University in England. They make a good contrast not only because of the personalities of the architects, but also because of the differing nature of their briefs. In Rudolph's case, the brief was to the best of my knowledge written by Rudolph (if it wasn't written by Scully). Rudolph was his own client, and if you put it that way, the process of confrontation between architect and program became almost purely one of introspection. Rudolph's response to the business of teaching and practicing architecture revolves very largely around the practice of draftsmanship, and the ritual of the criticism, and so the building, to a large extent, is a complex of drafting rooms around a central crit-pit or bear-baiting area or whatever you would call it. This sounds like a very simple proposition but, as we know, there were seven revisions of the design, partly because there was time, I suspect, to make them—lucky old Rudolph—partly because he was not clear in his own mind, perhaps because he had insufficient outside terms of reference against which to test his ideas. He had always to come back to what he thought and felt inside himself about how the building should be; and what you have got in the end is a building whose structure and symbolism are very difficult to take apart. It is one of the very few buildings I know which, when photographed, was exactly like a drawing, with all the shading on the outside coming out as if it were ruled in with a very soft pencil. It is a building *about* draftsmanship as surely as many English eighteenth-century Palladian buildings are, with their carefully pick-toothed rustication with the actual pattern of the design taken directly from the engravings in the *Quattro Libri*. So that it is a building *for* draftsmanship and a building conceived *in terms of* draftsmanship.

The Stirling and Gowan job at Leicester is a building about engineering and apparently considered in terms of engineering, but the process of design is very dissimilar to Rudolph's. For one thing, there were practically no revisions because there was no time. The building had to be finalized and the design had to be stabilized very early, and there was only one major revision of the design (and that of a literally superficial character), that is to say the change from large panes for glazing to a small standard industrial glazing system. The only major changes in the design were in the sketch stage; the pre-history of the building is all in the pre-drawing-board stage; the endless discussion of the brief, beginning with the situation in which the brief itself didn't exist—because they were working for a department which did not exist, for which not even a professor had been appointed at that particular stage. They had to start from examining what, in general terms, would be put on the site and by examining what had been done in other engineering departments, because they knew roughly what kinds of engineering would have to be taught. The process of discussion proceeded very rapidly indeed (partly because it had to), and the finalization of the design then proceeded very swiftly.

The completed building exhibits strong industrial characteristics, but to a large extent these are not obviously of symbolic value. The building, so to speak, has engineering written all over it, so that you recognize at once what sort of thing is supposed to be going on inside. But the symbolic expression was only in a very limited sense at the will of the architects; clearly the use of industrial glazing, for instance, was practically forced on them by economics, by a very tight budget, but they saw that it could be exploited to enhance and strengthen the symbolic expression of the building. It seems to me that the *intent* of both these buildings is something the critic needs to know, and he needs to explain this kind of process before he can really come to an effective value judgment about it. It is no use looking at Rudolph's building at Yale and saying: "I don't like it personally"—it is not enough to just say that. An opinion like that has got to be justified in depth and in detail. Again, it is not enough to say of the Stirling building at Leicester: "I think that is a jolly form; it is *copied* right?" As far as one can make out, it is functionally right, even though it does look formalistic, and all the worry about its forms and origins deals purely with epiphenomenal matters, if not irrelevancies.

One can examine other buildings in this existentialist situation, and still not come up with an opinion of approval. An example which you don't know because it hasn't been published yet, is the new building for the *Times* in London. Intellectually one can justify everything about that building as a resolution of an incredibly difficult, complex and in some stages very badly-worded or badly-thought-out original *Times* brief. But no one likes the look of the building. It will have no influence because no architect will be bothered to imitate it. And yet it is a building which on functional grounds is utterly and completely justifiable and on functional grounds deserves to be imitated. At any rate, the kind of intellectual approach deserves to be imitated.

Again, like many people, I panned the TWA building when I first saw it, or at least when I first saw the bare shell without anything inside. It did seem the most grotesque and gruesome piece of formalism, to create this sort of bald-headed eagle plonked on the side of the airfield there. It seemed the most awful piece of empty symbolism, of styling almost, and yet increasing acquaintance with that building convinces me more and more of Saarinen's functional understanding of the programme, both in terms of its physical and its symbolic (or psychological) functions. In the understanding of its functions, that building is almost impeccable. Particularly psychologically, it is one of the very few un-boring air terminals in the United States. There are many buildings which look far more functiional, like O'Hare International in Chicago, which is in terms of its design very straight and very simple. But you walk for miles in those corridors in search of a cigar-stand or a luncheon-station or even in search of an airplane. There are thousands of airplanes outside the window but which one is yours? In terms of psychological functions it is a disaster, you are frayed out, or too late, by the time you find what you want. Yet simply to go through that arching curve, that completely windowless corridor at TWA, is an utterly different experience and, looking back on it now, psychologically as clever as all get out! It really is so obviously a right way to deal with the problem; to show you the airplane from the concourse and then hide it from you until you get to

it. That slight arching in the floor may or may not be structurally necessary, but it makes the process of moving from here
to there not simply a number of steps; the fact that some of
the steps are up and some of the steps are down makes it an
interesting walk. I think that building is an extraordinary success but, as I say, one's immediate response was: "How dare he!
What the hell! I don't like the look of it!"

Now this clearly does pose some very serious problems because
architects are committed to be artists among other things. They
are charged with the business of making expressive visual symbols of this, that and the other, be it TWA, or the Glories of
the Soviet Union, or Mr. Blandings and his aspirations to build
a dream house, and because of their skill or expertise in the
creation and handling of symbolic visual expressions, they will
tend to accept or to decry buildings on that simple basis. The
old guard in France, who damned Le Corbusier's early buildings
before they knew anything about them functionally, damned
them because they didn't like the looks of them. They invented
functional reasons why they didn't work, but basically they took
against their symbolic expression. We all tend to do this. A
great number of plausible building solutions have got lost in the
rush, simply because people didn't like the looks of them; most
probably because certain influential teachers and certain influential editors didn't like the looks of them.

But God help us, every pedagogue is a human being, or so
they tell me, and human beings unavoidably have irrational pref-
erences and dislikes and so forth, which are bound to come over
in the teaching process. Part of the business of being an architect
and/or architectural critic is that you are dealing among other
things (and I insist on "among other things"), you are dealing
with visual symbols which are acceptable or not acceptable, for
fashionable reasons, for personal reasons, irrespective of the
functions that the building has to serve, and are the reasons why
it was built. And so I feel convinced that had Suzanne Langer
been an architect rather than the inventor of the systematic study
of visual symbols, she would probably have said that it was
symbolic expression and not utility which was the affliction of
architecture.

INDEX